Pocket

KYOTO & OSAKA

TOP SIGHTS · LOCAL LIFE · MADE EASY

Kate Morgan, Rebecca Milner

In This Book

QuickStart Guide

Your keys to understanding the cities – we help you decide what to do and how to do it

Need to Know
Tips for a smooth trip

Neighbourhoods
What's where

Explore Kyoto & Osaka

The best things to see and do, neighbourhood by neighbourhood

Top Sights
Make the most of your visit

Local Life
The insider's city

The Best of Kyoto & Osaka

The cities' highlights in handy lists to help you plan

Best Walks
See the city on foot

Kyoto & Osaka's Best...
The best experiences

Survival Guide

Tips and tricks for a seamless, hassle-free experience

Getting Around
Travel like a local

Essential Information
Including where to stay

Our selection of the best places to eat, drink and experience:

◎ **Sights**

✖ **Eating**

🍷 **Drinking**

✪ **Entertainment**

🔒 **Shopping**

These symbols give you the vital information for each listing:

✆ Telephone Numbers	♿ Family-Friendly
⏱ Opening Hours	🐾 Pet-Friendly
🅿 Parking	🚌 Bus
🚭 Nonsmoking	⛴ Ferry
@ Internet Access	Ⓜ Metro
🛜 Wi-Fi Access	Ⓢ Subway
🥗 Vegetarian Selection	⊖ London Tube
📖 English-Language	🚋 Tram
Menu	🚆 Train

Find each listing quickly on maps for each neighbourhood:

Bar Hemingway

16 🍷 Map p233, B2

Legend has it that Hemi self, wielding a machine rate this timber-pan ered bar during showpiece is a en by Papa ar town. Dress s.com; Hôtel Rit ⏱6.30pm-2a

6 ◎ Plac V

Lonely Planet's Kyoto and Osaka

Lonely Planet Pocket Guides are designed to get you straight to the heart of a city.

Inside you'll find all the must-see sights, plus tips to make your visit to each one really memorable. We've split each city into easy-to-navigate neighbourhoods and provided clear maps so you'll find your way around with ease. Our expert writers have searched out the best of the cities: walks, food, nightlife and shopping, to name a few. Because you want to explore, our 'Local Life' pages will take you to some of the most exciting areas to experience the real Kyoto and Osaka.

And of course you'll find all the practical tips you need for a smooth trip: itineraries for short visits, how to get around, and how much to tip the guy who serves you a drink at the end of a long day's exploration.

It's your guarantee of a really great experience.

Our Promise

You can trust our travel information because Lonely Planet authors visit the places we write about, each and every edition. We never accept freebies for positive coverage, so you can rely on us to tell it like it is.

The Best of Kyoto & Osaka 141

Kyoto & Osaka's Best Walks

Kyoto & Osaka's Best ...

Survival Guide 163

QuickStart Guide

Welcome to Kyoto & Osaka

Kyoto is old Japan writ large: quiet temples, sublime gardens, colourful shrines, postcard-perfect street scenes and geisha scurrying to secret liaisons. While Osaka's grey concrete jungle is no match in terms of beauty, this fast-paced, brash city cloaked in dazzling neon packs a punch with its excellent food and nightlife scenes, and locals full of personality.

Maiko (apprentice geisha; p68)
JORDI PRAT PUIG/SHUTTERSTOCK ©

Kyoto & Osaka
Top Sights

Kinkaku-ji (p90)

This is one of the world's most impressive religious monuments. The image of Kyoto's gold-plated pavilion rising over its reflecting pool is the kind that burns itself into your memory.

Gion (p62)

Gion is Kyoto's famous entertainment and geisha quarter on the eastern bank of the Kamo-gawa. The best way to experience it is with an evening stroll around the atmospheric streets lined with 17th-century traditional restaurants and teahouses.

Fushimi Inari-Taisha (p24)

With seemingly endless arcades of vermilion *torii* (shrine gates) spread across a thickly wooded mountain, this vast shrine complex in Kyoto is a world unto its own.

Nanzen-ji (p76)

This Zen temple in Kyoto has it all: a fine little *kare-sansui* (dry landscape) garden, soaring main halls, great gardens and an incredibly scenic location.

Kiyomizu-dera (p58)

One of Kyoto's most popular temples has attracted pilgrims since the 8th century AD. Wander the halls admiring fine Buddhist images and buy a prayer plaque at the shrine to assure success in romance.

Ginkaku-ji (p78)

Kyoto's famed Silver Pavilion is an enclosed paradise of ponds, thick moss, classical Japanese architecture and swaying bamboo groves.

Nishiki Market (p36)

Referred to as *Kyoto no daidokoro* (Kyoto's Kitchen) by locals, this is one of the city's highlights and is the place to discover all of the ingredients that go into Kyoto cuisine.

Chion-in (p60)

A collection of soaring buildings and spacious courtyards, Chion-in is the most popular pilgrimage temple in Kyoto and it's always a hive of religious activity.

Dōtombori (p110)

Highly photogenic Dōtombori is Osaka's liveliest night spot, with billboards glittering off its waters and dozens of restaurants jostling for attention with the most outrageous signage.

Kyoto Imperial Palace & Imperial Palace Park (p94)

Although no longer the emperor's residence, this park and palace recall the city's proud heritage as the seat of the imperial court for over 1000 years.

OLIVER FOERSTNER/SHUTTERSTOCK ©

LEWIS LIU/SHUTTERSTOCK ©

PALTEAVLAGMOV/SHUTTERSTOCK ©

COWARDLION/SHUTTERSTOCK ©

Nijō-jō (p38)

A stunning monument to the power of the warlords who effectively ruled Japan for centuries, Kyoto's Nijō-jō has superb interiors and the grounds contain expansive gardens that are perfect for a stroll.

Osaka-jō (p124)

Although the present structure is a reconstruction, Osaka-jō is an imposing castle and is nonetheless quite a sight, looming dramatically over the surrounding park and moat.

Kyoto & Osaka
Local Life

Insider tips to help you find the real cities

Once you've visited the temples, shrines and museums of Kyoto and Osaka, leave yourself enough time to hit up some of the spots most loved by locals – from evening strolls in atmospheric quarters and lazing in parks to tasting local beer in bars and shopping for traditional arts and crafts.

An Afternoon of Shopping, Kyoto (p40)

▶ Department and speciality stores

▶ Tea and dessert pit stops

Downtown's Nakagyō-ku area is Kyoto's beating heart of consumerism, where locals head to shop at the best boutiques and department stores, pick up gourmet goods from the Nishiki Market and to drop in for a casual lunch in between.

A Night on the Town, Kyoto (p42)

▶ Hidden local spots

▶ Atmospheric streets

While the area around Ponto-chō and Kiyamachi-dōri may be swarming with tourists at night, this is still very much an area favoured by locals for an evening out – from drinking in hidden-away bars to hanging out on the banks of the Kamo-gawa.

Parks, Tradition & Cafe Life, Kyoto (p96)

▶ Parks and gardens

▶ Traditional areas

The area around the Imperial Palace Park is where locals escape to for early morning jogs, while families head to the Botanical Gardens, and people go about their daily routine at home in their *machiya* (traditional Japanese townhouse) in Nishijin.

Shin-Sekai, Osaka (p112)

▶ Retro charm

▶ Cheap eats

A century ago, Shin-Sekai ('new world') was home to an amusement park that defined cutting edge. Now this entertainment district mixes down-on-its-heels with retro cool. It's got ancient (and a little sketchy) *pachinko* (pinball-style game) and mah-jong parlours, but also cheap and fun restaurants, a nostalgic mid-20th-century atmosphere and a big bathing complex.

Jogger in Kyoto Imperial Palace Park (p95)

Street in Shin-Sekai (p112), with Tsūten-kaku in the background

Other great places to experience the cities like a local:

Umeda Hagakure (p134)

Kyoto Brewing Company (p31)

Shunsai Tempura Arima (p46)

Salon de Amanto Tenjin (p137)

Kasagi-ya (p70)

Beer Komachi (p72)

Triangle Park (p116)

Karako (p86)

Misono Building (p120)

Kamiji Kakimoto (p55)

Kyoto & Osaka
Day Planner

Day One, Kyoto

☀ Start your Kyoto experience by heading to the city's most important sightseeing district: Southern Higashiyama contains the thickest concentration of worthwhile sights in Kyoto. Kick off with **Chion-in** (p60) and **Shoren-in** (p66) before a wander through **Maruyama-kōen** (p66). Head to **Hisago** (p70) for lunch – go for the house speciality, *oyako-donburi* (chicken and egg over rice).

☼ Walk off lunch with a stroll through the lanes of **Ninen-zaka and Sannen-zaka** (p69), stopping in at teahouses and boutiques. Afterwards, visit one of the city's premier sights, **Kiyomizu-dera** (p58). Spend the afternoon fully exploring this delightful temple.

☾ Perfect for dinner in this area is **Sobadokoro Shibazaki** (p70), with sushi and filling bowls of noodles, and a fine lacquerware gallery. After dinner you'll want to spend your first evening taking in the atmospheric **Gion** (p62) district and keeping an eye out for geisha shuffling around the traditional lantern-lit streets. Round off the evening with a drink at the **Gion Finlandia Bar** (p72).

Day Two, Kyoto

☀ There's a lot of ground to cover and a number of excellent temples to explore in Northern Higashiyama. Beat the crowds with an early visit to **Ginkaku-ji** (p78) before making your way along the **Path of Philosophy** (p82) to the splendid **Eikan-dō** (p82) temple and exploring the vast **Nanzen-ji** (p76) temple complex and gardens. Fuel up on a tasty bowl of noodles at **Hinode Udon** (p88).

☼ Take a break from temples and head to the Downtown area to check out the famous **Nishiki Market** (p40); don't miss the world-renowned chef's knives for sale at **Aritsugu** (p52). Carry on shopping in this area along the Teramachi covered arcade and the department stores on Kawaramachi-dōri and Shijo-dōri.

☾ Try the delicious delicacy *unagi* (eel) at **Kyōgoku Kane-yo** (p48) for dinner and then make your way to atmospheric **Ponto-chō** (p46). Stop in for a drink or grab a takeaway beer at the nearest convenience store and head for the Kamo-gawa to hang out riverside.

Short on time?
We've arranged Kyoto and Osaka's must-sees into these day-by-day itineraries to make sure you see the very best of the cities in the time you have available.

Day Three, Kyoto

☀ While the immediate Kyoto Station area doesn't offer much in the way of sightseeing, head a little further south to see two absolutely stunning attractions: **Tōfuku-ji** (p28; don't forget to enter the Hōjō garden) and **Fushimi Inari-Taisha** (p24). Head back to the station to marvel at the architecture if you haven't taken time to do this already. For lunch, take your pick of nine ramen restaurants at **Kyoto Rāmen Kōji** (p30) inside Kyoto Station.

☀ From Kyoto Station, jump on a bus bound for **Kinkaku-ji** (p90), one of Japan's most well-known sights. Admire the temple and check out the Zen garden before heading to Southern Higashiyama to wander around some more peaceful Zen temples, such as **Kōdai-ji** (p67).

☽ Tasty udon with fresh vegetables at **Omen Kodai-ji** (p70) await for dinner, then head over to **Beer Komachi** (p72) to knock back Japanese craft beer and mingle with the locals.

Day Four, Osaka

☀ Start with a visit to **Osaka-jō** (p125); swing by **Gout** (p125) for pastries on the way, to eat on the castle lawns. Take time to explore the surrounding grounds, castle interiors and observation deck. From here, take the Tanimachi subway line to Higashi-Umeda, to pay your respects to star-crossed lovers Ohatsu and Tokubei at **O-hatsu Ten-jin** (p132). Stop for an *okonomiyaki* (savoury pancake) lunch at nearby **Yukari** (p133).

☀ Take the subway down to Shinsaibashi, to stroll through **Shinsaibashi-suji Shōtengai** (p122) and over **Ebisu-bashi** (p111) before joining the nightly throngs in neon-lit **Dōtombori** (p118).

☽ There are plenty of places to eat around Dōtombori, such as **Imai Honten** (p117). Once you've had your fill of food and flashing neon, walk over to **Amerika-Mura** (p115), which is full of bars and clubs, to finish the night off dancing and drinking with the locals.

Need to Know

For more information, see Survival Guide (p163)

Currency
Japanese yen (¥)

Language
Japanese

Visas
Visas are issued on arrival for most nationalities for stays of up to 90 days.

Money
ATMs available in major banks, post offices and 7-Eleven stores. Credit cards accepted in most hotels and department stores, but only some restaurants and ryokan.

Mobile Phones
Purchase prepaid data-only SIM cards (for unlocked smartphones only) online, at airport kiosks or at electronics stores. For voice calls, rent a pay-as-you-go mobile.

Time
Local time is nine hours ahead of GMT/UTC. There is no daylight-saving time.

Plugs & Adaptors
Electrical current is 100V AC; two flat pins with no earth.

Tipping
Tipping is not usually done in Japan.

① Before You Go

Your Daily Budget

Budget: Less than ¥10,000
- ▶ Guesthouse accommodation: ¥3000
- ▶ Two simple restaurant meals: ¥2200
- ▶ Train/bus transport: ¥1500
- ▶ One temple/museum admission: ¥500

Midrange: ¥10,000–20,000
- ▶ Business-hotel accommodation: ¥10,000
- ▶ Two midrange restaurant meals: ¥5000
- ▶ Train/bus transport: ¥1500
- ▶ Two temple/museum admissions: ¥1000

Top End: More than ¥20,000
- ▶ First-class hotel accommodation: ¥25,000
- ▶ Two good restaurant meals: ¥8000
- ▶ Train/bus transport: ¥1500
- ▶ Two taxi rides: ¥3500

Useful Websites

- ▶ **Lonely Planet** (www.lonelyplanet.com/kyoto) Destination info, traveller forum etc.
- ▶ **Kyoto Visitor's Guide** (www.kyotoguide.com) Great all-around Kyoto info.
- ▶ **HyperDia** (www.hyperdia.com/en/) Train schedules in English.

Advance Planning

Several months before Make accommodation reservations if you're here in cherry-blossom season (March and April) and the autumn-foliage season (October and November).

One month before Buy a Japan Rail Pass if you'll be travelling extensively by rail in Japan.

A few days before Buy a pair of comfortable slip-on walking shoes (you'll be taking your shoes off a lot at temples and shrines).

2 Arriving in Kyoto & Osaka

✈ Arriving by Air

Kyoto Kansai International Airport (KIX) is Kyoto's main international entry point. Built on an artificial island in Osaka Bay, it's about 75 minutes away from Kyoto by direct express trains.

Osaka Two airports serve Osaka: Kansai International Airport for all international and some domestic flights; and the domestic Itami Airport, also confusingly called Osaka International Airport. KIX is about 50km southwest of the city, Itami is 12km northwest of Osaka.

🚆 Arriving by Train

Kyoto Kyoto Station is linked to nearby cities by several excellent train lines, including Japan Railways (JR). JR also has links to cities further afield, many of which are served by super-fast *shinkansen* (bullet trains).

Osaka Shin-Osaka Station is on the Tōkaidō-Sanyō *shinkansen* line. Departures are frequent to many main Japanese cities.

Regular trains run between Osaka and Kyoto and include the JR Kyoto line from Osaka Station to Kyoto (¥560, 28 minutes) and the Hankyū Kyoto line. Tokkyū (limited express) trains run from Hankyū Umeda Station to Karasuma (¥400, 40 minutes) and Kawara-machi (¥400, 44 minutes) in Kyoto.

3 Getting Around

Kyoto

🚆 Train & Subway

Kyoto has two efficient subway lines, operating from 5.30am to 11.30pm. Minimum adult fare is ¥210. It gets you quickly between north and south (the Karasuma line) or east and west (the Tōzai line). In addition to the private Kintetsu train line that operates from Kyoto Station, there are two other private lines: the Hankyū line that operates from Downtown Kyoto and the Keihan line that operates from stops along the Kamo-gawa.

🚌 Bus

Kyoto has an intricate network of bus routes providing an efficient way of getting around at moderate cost. Many of the routes used by visitors have announcements in English. Most buses run between 7am and 9pm.

🚲 Bicycle

Kyoto is a great city to explore on a bicycle. It's mostly flat and there is a useful bike path running the length of the Kamo-gawa.

Osaka

🚆 Train & Subway

The JR Kanjō-sen – the Osaka loop line – makes a circuit south of JR Osaka Station, though most sights fall in the middle of it. There are eight subway lines, but the one that short-term visitors will find most useful is the Midō-suji (red) line, running north–south and stopping at Shin-Osaka, Umeda (next to Osaka Station), Shinsaibashi, Namba and Tennōji stations. Single rides cost ¥180 to ¥370.

🚌 Bus

Osaka has an extensive bus system (rides ¥210), but train and subway are easier to use.

🚕 Taxi

Taxis are your only option after midnight. Flagfall is ¥680, which covers the first 2km; then it's ¥80 for every additional 266m or 100 seconds stuck in traffic.

Kyoto Neighbourhoods

Northern Higashiyama (p74)

Loaded with top-rate sightseeing options – from temples and shrines to art museums, with impossibly scenic canal pathways and parks in between.

⊙ Top Sights

Nanzen-ji

Ginkaku-ji

Imperial Palace & Around (p92)

The greenest part of the city, where locals come to unwind, with expansive parks, Zen-temple complexes and imperial historical sights.

⊙ Top Sights

Kyoto Imperial Palace & Imperial Palace Park

Downtown Kyoto (p34)

Trade your temple-hopping for shopping before dining and drinking your way around the city's best bars and eateries.

⊙ Top Sights

Nishiki Market

Nijō-jō

Kyoto Station & South Kyoto (p22)

While it may be the transport hub of the city, this neighbourhood surprises with sights such as stunning shrine complexes and tucked-away temples.

⊙ Top Sight

Fushimi Inari-Taisha

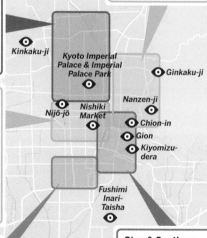

Kinkaku-ji

Kyoto Imperial Palace & Imperial Palace Park

Ginkaku-ji

Nanzen-ji

Nijō-jō

Nishiki Market

Chion-in

Gion

Kiyomizu-dera

Fushimi Inari-Taisha

Worth a Trip

⊙ Top Sights

Kinkaku-ji (p90)

◯ Local Life

Arashiyama (p106)

Gion & Southern Higashiyama (p56)

Here, geisha shuffle down alleyways, temples enchant visitors and traditional tea shops are scattered about.

⊙ Top Sights

Kiyomizu-dera

Chion-in

Gion

Osaka
Neighbourhoods

Worth a Trip

⊙ Top Sights

Osaka-jō (p124)

Tōdai-ji & Nara-kōen (p126)

Kita (p128)
The working heart of the city, skyscraper-filled Kita is the transport and business hub of Osaka, with some good shopping, shrines and the art museum hidden in amongst the bustle.

⊙ *Osaka-jō*

Minami (p108)
The antidote to straight-laced Kita, this is where Osakans come to let their hair down amid flashing neon, late-night bars and some of the city's best shopping arcades.

⊙ Top Sight

Dōtombori

Dōtombori **⊙**

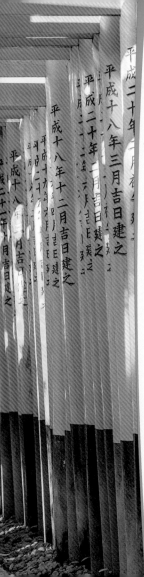

Explore
Kyoto & Osaka

Worth a Trip

Women strolling at Fushimi Inari-Taisha (p24), Kyoto
OLIVER FOERSTNER/SHUTTERSTOCK ©

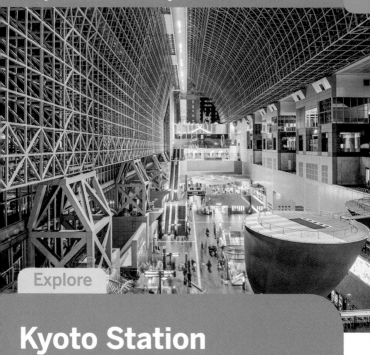

Explore

Kyoto Station & South Kyoto

Dominated by Kyoto Station, this neighbourhood serves as the gateway to Kyoto. There are a couple of temples within walking distance of the station, and the excellent Railway Museum is a short bus ride away. Venture further south and you've got one of the city's most stunning attractions, the Shintō-shrine complex Fushimi Inari-Taisha, as well as the superb Tōfuku-ji temple and garden.

SEAN PAVONE/SHUTTERSTOCK ©

The Sights in a Day

☀ Beat the crowds and start your day with an early morning visit to the ethereal **Fushimi Inari-Taisha** (p24). Hike across the sprawling shrine complex before heading to **Vermillion** (p31) for a well-deserved coffee. Next stop is the serene gardens and stunning Buddhist temple of **Tōfuku-ji** (p28) before catching the train back to **Kyoto Station** (p28) to marvel at its architecture.

☀ For lunch, take your pick of nine ramen restaurants at **Kyoto Rāmen Kōji** (p30) inside Kyoto Station, then make your way across the street to zip up the **Kyoto Tower** (p30) for views across the city. Jump on a bus bound for the excellent, interactive **Kyoto Railway Museum** (p29), where you can check out the collection of vintage steam locomotives before taking a ride on one.

☾ Make your way back to Kyoto Station and wander north to admire the massive Buddhist temples of **Nishi Hongan-ji** (p29) and **Higashi Hongan-ji** (p28), and take some time out in the peaceful **Shōsei-en** (p30) gardens. Peruse the collection of restaurants at **Cube** (p31) and **Eat Paradise** (p31) to decide on dinner, and hit the **shops** (p31) afterwards to stock up on electronics.

👁 **Top Sight**

Fushimi Inari-Taisha (p24)

💜 **Best of Kyoto**

Eating

Kyoto Rāmen Kōji (p30)

Eat Paradise (p31)

Cube (p31)

Shopping

Bic Camera (p31)

Yodobashi Camera (p32)

Isetan (p32)

Getting There

🚃 **Train** The JR lines, including the *shinkansen* (bullet train), and the private Kintetsu line operate to/from Kyoto Station.

🚌 **Bus** Many city buses, JR buses and other bus lines operate to/from the Kyoto Station Bus Terminal (on the north side of the station).

Ⓢ **Subway** The Karasuma subway line stops directly underneath Kyoto Station (the Kyoto Station stop is called simply 'Kyoto').

Top Sights
Fushimi Inari-Taisha

With seemingly endless arcades of vermilion *torii* (shrine gates) spread across a thickly wooded mountain, this vast shrine complex is a world unto its own. It is, quite simply, one of the most impressive and memorable sights in all of Kyoto. A pathway wanders 4km up the mountain and is lined with dozens of atmospheric sub-shrines.

伏見稲荷大社

Map p26, H5

68 Yabunouchi-chō, Fukakusa, Fushimi-ku

admission free

⏱dawn-dusk

🚉JR Nara line to Inari or Keihan line to Fushimi-Inari

Fox statue

Background

Fushimi Inari was dedicated to the gods of rice and sake by the Hata family in the 8th century. As the role of agriculture diminished, deities were enrolled to ensure prosperity in business. Nowadays the shrine is one of Japan's most popular, and is the head shrine for some 40,000 Inari shrines scattered the length and breadth of the country.

The Messenger of Inari

As you explore the shrine, you will come across hundreds of stone foxes. The fox is considered the messenger of Inari, the god of cereals, and the stone foxes, too, are often referred to as Inari. The key often seen in the fox's mouth is for the rice granary. On an incidental note, the Japanese traditionally see the fox as a sacred, some-what mysterious figure capable of 'possessing' humans – the favoured point of entry is under the fingernails.

Hiking

The walk around the upper precincts of the shrine is a pleasant day hike. It also makes for a very eerie stroll in the late afternoon and early evening, when the various graveyards and miniature shrines along the path take on a myste-rious air. It's best to go with a friend at this time.

☑ **Top Tips**

▶ Don't be afraid to get lost – that's part of the fun at Fushimi.

▶ A good time to visit is in the first few days of January to see thousands of believers visit this shrine as their *hatsu-mōde* (first shrine visit of the New Year) to pray for good fortune.

▶ Come on 8 April to witness the Sangyō-sai festival, when offerings are made and dances performed to ensure prosperity for national industry.

✕ **Take a Break**

Vermillion (p31) cafe is the perfect place to take a rest after exploring the shrine complex. It serves excellent coffee and cakes.

QUALITY STOCK ARTS/SHUTTERSTOCK ©

A B C D

1

0 — 200 m
0 — 0.1 miles

Nishi Hongan-ji ◉5

Omiya-dōri

SHIMOGYŌ-KU

Shichijō-dōri

2

Horikawa-dōri

◉6
Kyoto Railway Museum

Kitsuyabashi-dōri

Kitsuyabashi-dōri

Umekōji-kōen

Omiya-dōri

3

Hachijo-dōri

Hachijō-dōri

4

Harikoji-dōri

For reviews see	
◉ Top Sights	p24
◎ Sights	p28
✖ Eating	p30
🍷 Drinking	p31
🛍 Shopping	p31

Tōji-dōri

Tō-ji
3 ◎
15 🛍

Omiya-dōri

Inokuma-dōri

🚈 Tōji

MINAMI-KU

5

Kyoto Brewing Company (700m) ↓

Sights

Tōfuku-ji
BUDDHIST TEMPLE

1 ◎ Map p26, H5

Home to a spectacular garden, several superb structures and beautiful precincts, Tōfuku-ji is one of the best temples in Kyoto. It's well worth a visit and can easily be paired with a trip to Fushimi Inari-Taisha (the temples are linked by the Keihan and JR train lines). The present temple complex includes 24 subtemples. The huge San-mon is the oldest Zen main gate in Japan, the Hōjō (Abbot's Hall) was reconstructed in 1890, and the gardens were laid out in 1938. (東福寺; 📞075-561-0087; 15-778 Honmahi, Higashiyama-ku; Hōjō garden ¥400, Tsūten-kyō bridge ¥400; ⏱9am-4pm mid-Dec–Oct, 8.30am-4.30pm Nov-early Dec; 🚃Keihan line to Tōfukuji or JR Nara line to Tōfukuji)

Kyoto Station
NOTABLE BUILDING

2 ◎ Map p26, F3

The Kyoto Station building is a striking steel-and-glass structure – a kind of futuristic cathedral for the transport age – with a tremendous space that arches above you as you enter the main concourse. Be sure to take the escalator from the 7th floor on the east side of the building up to the 11th-floor glass corridor, Skyway (open 10am to 10pm), that runs high above the main concourse of the station, and catch some views from the 15th-floor Sky Garden terrace. (京都駅; www.kyoto-station-building.co.jp; Karasuma-dōri, Higashishiokōji-chō, Shiokōji-sagaru, Shimogyō-ku; 🚃Kyoto Station)

Tō-ji
BUDDHIST TEMPLE

3 ◎ Map p26, B5

One of the sights south of Kyoto Station, Tō-ji is an appealing complex of halls and a fantastic pagoda that makes a fine backdrop for the monthly flea market (p32) held on the grounds. The temple was established in 794 by imperial decree to protect the city. In 823 the emperor handed it over to Kūkai (known posthumously as Kōbō Daishi), the founder of the Shingon school of Buddhism. (東寺; 1 Kujō-chō, Minami-ku; admission to grounds free, Kondō & Kōdō ¥500 each, pagoda, Kondō & Kōdō ¥800; ⏱8.30am-5pm 20 Mar-19 Sep, to 4pm 20 Sep-19 Mar; 🚃Kyoto City bus 205 from Kyoto Station, 🚃Kintetsu Kyoto line to Tōji)

Higashi Hongan-ji
BUDDHIST TEMPLE

4 ◎ Map p26, F1

A short walk north of Kyoto Station, Higashi Hongan-ji is the last word in all things grand and gaudy. Considering its proximity to the station, the free admission, the awesome structures and the dazzling interiors, this temple is the obvious spot to visit when near the station. The temple is dominated by the vast **Goei-dō** hall, said to be the second-largest wooden structure in Japan, standing 38m high, 76m long and 58m wide. (東本願寺, Eastern Temple of the True Vow; Karasuma-dōri, Shichijō-agaru, Shimogyō-ku; audio guide

GORAN BOGICEVIC/SHUTTERSTOCK ©

Kyoto Railway Museum

at information centre ¥500; ⏲5.50am-5.30pm Mar-Oct, 6.20am-4.30pm Nov-Feb; 🚉Kyoto Station)

Nishi Hongan-ji BUDDHIST TEMPLE

5 ◎ Map p26, D1

A vast temple complex located about 15 minutes' walk northwest of Kyoto Station, Nishi Hongan-ji comprises five buildings that feature some of the finest examples of architecture and artistic achievement from the Azuchi-Momoyama period (1568–1600). The **Goei-dō** (Main Hall) is a marvellous sight. Another must-see building is the **Daisho-in** hall, which has sumptuous paintings, carvings and metal ornamentation. A small garden and two *nō* (stylised Japanese dance-drama) stages are connected with the hall. The dazzling **Kara-mon** has intricate ornamental carvings. (西本願寺; Horikawa-dōri, Hanayachō-sagaru, Shimogyō-ku; admission free; ⏲5.30am-5pm Nov-Feb, to 5.30pm Mar, Apr, Sep & Oct, to 6pm May-Aug; 🚉Kyoto Station)

Kyoto Railway Museum MUSEUM

6 ◎ Map p26, A2

The Umekoji Steam Locomotive Museum underwent a massive expansion in 2016 to reopen as the Kyoto Railway Museum. This superb museum is spread over three floors showcasing 53 trains, from vintage steam locomotives in the outside Roundhouse Shed to commuter trains and the first *shinkansen* (bullet train) from 1964. Kids will love the interactive displays and impressive railroad diorama with miniature trains zipping through the intricate landscape. You can also take a 10-minute ride on one of the smoke-spewing choo-choos. (梅小路蒸気機関車館; www.kyotorailwaymuseum.jp; Kankiji-chō, Shimogyō-ku; adult/child ¥1200/200, train ride ¥300/100; ◷10am-5.30pm, closed Wed; 🚌Kyoto City bus 103, 104 or 105 from Kyoto Station to Umekō-ji Kōen-mae)

Kyoto Tower NOTABLE BUILDING

7 Map p26, F2

Located right outside the Karasuma (north) gate of Kyoto Station, this retro tower looks like a rocket perched atop the Kyoto Tower Hotel. The tower provides excellent views in all directions and you can really get a sense for the Kyoto *bonchi* (flat basin). It's a great place to get orientated to the city upon arrival. There are free mounted binoculars to use and a cool touchscreen panel showing what the view looks like both day and night.

Top Tip

Snacks for the Train Trip

Porta (Map p26, F3), the shopping mall underneath the north side of Kyoto Station, is crammed with shops that sell takeaway food and snacks of all descriptions; perfect for when you're jumping on the train.

(京都タワー; Karasuma-dōri, Shichijō-sagaru, Shimogyō-ku; ¥770; ◷9am-9pm, last entry 8.40pm; 🚇Kyoto Station)

Shōsei-en GARDENS

8 Map p26, G1

About five minutes' walk east of Higashi Hongan-ji, this garden is a peaceful green island in a vast expanse of concrete. While it's not on par with many other gardens in Kyoto, it's worth a visit if you find yourself in need of something to do near Kyoto Station, perhaps paired with a visit to the temple. The lovely grounds, incorporating the **Kikoku-tei** villa, were completed in 1657. (渉成園; ☎075-371-9210; Karasuma-dōri, Shichijō-agaru, Shimogyō-ku; ¥500; ◷9am-5pm Mar-Oct, to 4pm Nov-Feb; 🚇Kyoto Station)

Eating

Kyoto Rāmen Kōji RAMEN ¥

9 🍴 Map p26, F3

If you love your noodles, do not miss this collection of nine ramen restaurants on the 10th floor of the Kyoto Station building (on the west end, take the escalators that start in the main concourse or access via the JR Isetan south elevator). Buy tickets from the machines (in English, with pictures) before queuing. (京都拉麺小路; ☎075-361-4401; www.kyoto-ramen-koji.com; 10F Kyoto Station Bldg, Karasuma-dōri, Shiokōji-sagaru, Shimogyō-ku; ramen ¥730-1150; ◷11am-10pm; 📶; 🚇Kyoto Station)

Eat Paradise

JAPANESE ¥

10 Map p26, F3

Up on the 11th floor of the Kyoto Station building, you'll find this collection of decent restaurants. Among the choices here are **Tonkatsu Wako** for *tonkatsu* (deep-fried breaded pork cutlet), **Tenichi** for sublime tempura, and **Wakuden** for approachable *kaiseki* (Japanese haute cuisine). (イートパラダイス; ☏075-352-1111; 11F Kyoto Station Bldg, Karasuma-dōri, Shiokōji-sagaru, Shimogyō-ku; ☺11am-10pm; 🖾; 🚉Kyoto Station)

Cube

JAPANESE ¥

11 Map p26, F3

This is a great collection of restaurants located on the 11th floor of the Kyoto Station building. Most of the restaurants here serve Japanese food. You'll see it on your left as you arrive by escalator on the 11th floor. (ザ キューブ; ☏075-371-2134; 11F Kyoto Station Bldg, Karasuma-dōri, Shiokōji-sagaru, Shimogyō-ku; ☺11am-10pm; 🖾; 🚉Kyoto Station)

Drinking

Vermillion Espresso Bar

CAFE

12 Map p26, H5

A Melbourne-inspired cafe, Vermillion takes its name from the colour of the *torii* gates of the nearby Fushimi Inari-Taisha shrine. It does standout coffee as well as a small selection of

cakes. It's on the main street, just a short hop from Inari Station. (バーミリオン; 85 Fukakusa-inari, Onmae-chō, Fushimi-ku; ☺10am-5.30pm Mon-Wed & Fri, 9am-5.30pm Sat & Sun; 🚉JR Nara line to Inari)

Shopping

Bic Camera

ELECTRONICS

13 🔒 Map p26, E3

This vast store is directly connected to Kyoto Station via the Nishinotō-in gate; otherwise, it's accessed by leaving the north (Karasuma) gate and walking west. The sheer amount of gadgets and goods this store has on display is amazing. Just be sure that an English operating manual is available for your purchases. (ビッ

Top Tip

Last-Minute Gifts

Isetan (ジェイアール京都伊勢丹; Map p26, F3; ☏075-352-1111; Kyoto Station Bldg, Karasuma-dōri, Shiokōji-sagaru, Shimogyō-ku; ⏰10am-8pm; 🚉Kyoto Station) is an elegant department store located inside the Kyoto Station building, making it perfect for a last-minute spot of shopping before hopping on the train to the airport. Don't miss the B1 and B2 food floors.

ク カ メ ラ; ☏075-353-1111; 927 Higashi Shiokōji-chō, Shimogyō-ku; ⏰10am-9pm; 🚉Kyoto Station)

Yodobashi Camera   ELECTRONICS

14 🔒 Map p26, F2

This mammoth shop sells a range of electronics, camera and computer goods, and also has a restaurant floor,

branch of popular Uniqlo budget clothing store, supermarket, bookshop, cafe and, well, the list goes on. It's a few minutes' walk north of Kyoto Station. (ヨ ドバシカメラ; ☏075-351-1010; 590-2 Higashi Shiokōji-chō, Shimogyō-ku; ⏰9.30am-10pm; 🚉Kyoto Station)

Kōbō-san Market   MARKET

15 🔒 Map p26, B5

This market is held at Tō-ji each month to commemorate the death of Kōbō Daishi, who in 823 was appointed abbot of the temple. If you're after used kimonos, pottery, bric-a-brac, plants, tools and general Japanalia, this is the place. (弘法さん, 東寺露天市; 1 Kujō-chō, Tō-ji, Minami-ku; ⏰dawn-dusk, 21st of each month; 🚌Kyoto City bus 205 from Kyoto Station, 🚉Kintetsu Kyoto line to Tōji)

Plates for sale at Kōbō-san Market

Explore

Downtown Kyoto

If all you're interested in on your Kyoto trip is dining on great cuisine, knocking back sake and craft beer at bars, boutique shopping and staying in some of the finest ryokan, you may just never leave Downtown Kyoto. And you wouldn't need to sacrifice culture or sightseeing, with heavyweight attractions such as Nijō-jō, the famed Nishiki Market and a smattering of small temples, shrines and museums.

The Sights in a Day

☀ Grab an expertly brewed coffee at stand-up cafe **Weekenders** (p50) before wandering the food stalls and stocking up on gourmet goods at **Nishiki Market** (p36). Continue the shopping at **Kyoto Design House** (p54), **Zōhiko** (p52) and **Ippōdō Tea** (p52) to pick up excellent gifts and souvenirs. When the hunger sets in, make your way to **Yoshikawa** (p48) for some of the city's best tempura.

☀ Spend most of your afternoon visiting **Nijō-jō** (p38) and stepping on its squeaking nightingale floors before heading back to the main shopping strips to go floor-to-floor at department stores **Takashimaya** (p54) and **Tokyu Hands** (p55), checking out gadgets and homewares.

☾ For dinner make sure you book ahead for sensational *kaiseki* at **Roan Kikunoi** (p48), then wander down the lantern-lit **Ponto-chō** (p42) area after dark before grabbing a cocktail or two at **Sama Sama** (p50) or craft beer at **Bungalow** (p50).

For a local's day in Downtown Kyoto, see p40, and for a local's night out, see p42.

👁 Top Sights
Nishiki Market (p36)

Nijō-jō (p38)

🔍 Local Life
An Afternoon of Shopping (p40)

A Night on the Town (p42)

💜 Best of Kyoto
Eating

Honke Owariya (p47)

Yoshikawa (p48)

Roan Kikunoi (p48)

Kyōgoku Kane-yo (p48)

Ippūdō (p49)

Shopping

Aritsugu (p52)

Zōhiko (p52)

Ippōdō Tea (p52)

Takashimaya (p54)

Wagami no Mise (p54)

Getting There

Ⓢ **Subway** Karasuma line to Shijō.

🚃 **Train** Hankyū line to Karasuma or Kawaramachi.

Top Sights
Nishiki Market

Nishiki Market (Nishiki-kōji Ichiba) is one of Kyoto's real highlights, especially if you have an interest in cooking and eating. Commonly known as *Kyoto no daidokoro* (Kyoto's kitchen) by locals, it's where most of Kyoto's high-end restaurateurs and wealthy individuals do their food shopping. This is the place to see the weird and wonderful foods that go into Kyoto cuisine.

錦市場

Map p44, F3

Nishikikōji-dōri, btwn Teramachi & Takakura, Nakagyō-ku

🕙9am-5pm

Ⓢ Karasuma line to Shijō, Ⓡ Hankyū line to Karasuma or Kawaramachi

Fresh produce at Nishiki Market

History

The pedestrian-only, covered Nishiki Market is right smack in the centre of town, one block north of Shijō-dōri, running from Teramachi shōtengai to Takakura-dōri (ending almost behind Daimaru department store). It's said that there were stores here as early as the 14th century, and it's known for sure that the street was a wholesale fish market in the Edo period (1603–1868). After the end of Edo, as Japan entered the modern era, the market became a retail market, which it remains today.

The Wares

The emphasis is on locally produced Japanese food items like *tsukemono* (Japanese pickles), tea, beans, rice, seaweed and fish (if you know how to read Japanese or know what to look for, you'll even see the odd bit of whale meat). In recent years the market has been evolving from a strictly local food market into a tourist attraction, and you'll now find several souvenir shops selling Kyoto-style souvenirs mixed in among the food stalls.

Shopping Highlight

Aritsugu (p52) turns out some of the most exquisite knives on earth. Take time to pick the perfect one for your needs, then watch as the craftsmen carefully put a final edge on the knife with the giant round sharpening stone – the end product will be so sharp it will scare you.

☑ Top Tips

▶ The market is quite narrow and can get elbow-to-elbow busy, so try visiting early or later in the afternoon if you prefer a bit of space.

▶ Some stores don't appreciate visitors taking photos, so it's a good idea to ask politely before snapping away.

✕ Take a Break

Grab a fresh fruit juice on the south side of the market at **Iketsuru Kajitsu** (池鶴果実; Nishikikōji-dōri, Yanaginobanba higashi-iru, Nakagyō-ku; juice ¥450; ⊙10am-6pm; ⓈKarasuma line to Shijō, ⓇHankyū line to Karasuma or Kawaramachi).

Queue up for some of the city's best ramen just steps from the market at Ippūdō (p49).

Top Sights
Nijō-jō

Standing like a direct challenge to the might of the emperor in the nearby Imperial Palace, the shogun castle of Nijō-jō (二条城) is a stunning monument to the power of the warlords who effectively ruled Japan for centuries. It's a fascinating destination, with superb (almost rococo) interiors, and the grounds contain expansive gardens that are perfect for a stroll.

Map p44, B1

541 Nijōjō-chō, Nijō-dōri, Horikawa nishi-iru, Nakagyō-ku

adult/child ¥600/200

🕘8.45am-5pm, Ninomaru palace 9am-4pm, closed Tue Dec, Jan, Jul & Aug

S Tōzai line to Nijō-jō-mae, R JR line to Nijō Station

Handcrafted features on the exterior of Nijō-jō

Background

In 1868 the last Tokugawa shogun, Yoshinobu, surrendered his power to the newly restored Emperor Meiji inside Nijō-jō.

Nijō-jō is built on land that was originally occupied by the 8th-century Imperial Palace, which was abandoned in 1227. The castle was constructed in 1603 as the official Kyoto residence of the first Tokugawa shogun, Ieyasu. To safeguard against treachery, Ieyasu had the interior fitted with 'nightingale' floors (intruders were detected by the squeaking boards) and concealed chambers where bodyguards could keep watch and spring out at a moment's notice.

The Shinsen-en Garden, just south of the castle, is all that remains of the original palace. This forlorn garden has small shrines and a pond.

Highlights

The **Momoyama-era Kara-mon gate**, originally part of Hideyoshi's Fushimi-jō in the south of the city, features lavish, masterful woodcarving and metalwork. After passing through the gate, you enter the **Ninomaru palace**, which is divided into five buildings with numerous chambers. Access to the buildings used to depend on rank – only those of highest rank were permitted into the inner buildings. The **Ōhiroma Yon-no-Ma** (Fourth Chamber) has spectacular screen paintings.

The neighbouring **Honmaru palace** dates from the mid-19th century. After the Meiji Restoration in 1868, the castle became a detached palace of the imperial household and in 1939 it was given to Kyoto City. These days it's only open for a special autumn viewing.

Seiryu-en, the garden that surrounds the inner castle buildings, is a must-see. Designed by Kobori Enshū, Japan's most celebrated garden designer, it is meticulously maintained. The Ninomaru palace and garden take about an hour to walk through. A detailed fact sheet in English is provided.

QUALITY STOCK ARTS/SHUTTERSTOCK ©

☑ **Top Tips**

▶ The castle is on the itinerary of every foreign and Japanese tour group and it can be packed. If you're after peace and quiet, try an early-morning or late-afternoon visit.

▶ To get more out of your visit, you can hire an audio guide for ¥500.

✕ **Take a Break**

Tuck into a homemade veggie burger, vegan cake and tasty coffee at Cafe Phalam (p49).

Local Life
An Afternoon of Shopping

This area is Kyoto's beating heart of consumerism, where locals head to shop at the best boutiques and departments stores, pick up gourmet goods from the Nishiki Market to cook at home, and to drop in for a casual lunch and coffee in between.

❶ Nishiki Market

Arrive early to beat the crowds at this wonderful market (p36), home to a bounty of ingredients that go into Kyoto's cuisine. Wander from stall to stall inspecting the gourmet goods, duck into shops selling spices and sweets, and grab a snack to go.

❷ Daimaru

Perhaps the best-known department store, you can really while away the hours at **Daimaru** (大丸; ☎075-211-8111; Tachiuri Nishi-machi 79, Shijō-dōri, Takakura nishi-iru, Shimogyō-ku; ⊙10am-8pm,

restaurants 11am-9pm; **S** Karasuma line to Shijō, **R** Hankyū line to Karasuma). Most of that time could be spent just checking out what's on offer in the basement food section, where locals head to pick up *bentō* boxes, sweets, tempura and sushi.

3 Tagoto Honten

Take a break at **Tagoto Honten** (田ごと本店; ☎075-221-1811; www.kyoto-tagoto.co.jp; 34 Otabi-chō, Shijō-dōri, Kawaramachi nishi-iru, Nakagyō-ku; lunch/dinner from ¥1850/4000; ⏱11am-8.30pm; ⓟ; **R** Keihan line to Shijō or Hankyū line to Kawaramachi), just across the street from Takashimaya, which is a magnet for shoppers in need of a feed. It's a great spot to sample affordable *kaiseki* (Japanese haute cuisine) in a lovely, quiet setting that has you forgetting the hustle of the main streets outside. Save room for dessert, though.

4 Mina

More shopping awaits at **Mina** (ミーナ京都; ☎075-222-8470; Kawaramachi-dōri, Shijō-agaru, Nakagyō-ku; ⏱11am-9pm; **R** Keihan line to Gion-Shijō or Hankyū line to Kawaramachi), a favourite for two of Japan's most popular chains: Uniqlo, a budget clothing brand that has spread overseas; and Loft, a fashionable department store that stocks all manner of gadgets and gift items. Take your time here moving from floor to floor, browsing everything from pottery and stationery to fashion and homewares.

5 Karafuneya Coffee Sanjō Honten

Hopefully your earlier *kaiseki* meal has left you just satisfied with room for more. A short walk away from Mina is **Karafuneya Coffee Sanjō Honten** (からふねや珈琲三条本店; ☎075-254-8774; 39 Daikoku-chō, Kawaramachi-dōri, Sanjō-sagaru, Nakagyō-ku; parfait from ¥690; ⏱9am-11pm; ⓟ; **S** Tōzai line to Kyoto-Shiyakusho-mae, **R** Keihan line to Sanjō), a local's favourite for light lunches and coffee but the real temptation is the huge selection of sundaes on the menu. Tuck into a *matcha* (powdered green tea) parfait or *azuki* (red bean) with black sesame.

6 Kaboku Tearoom

Walk off the dessert and make your way to this lovely **tearoom** (喫茶室嘉木; Teramachi-dōri, Nijō-agaru, Nakagyō-ku; tea from ¥600; ⏱10am-6pm; **S** Tōzai line to Kyoto-Shiyakusho-mae) to refresh yourself with a cup of tea. Choose from a range of green teas, including high-quality *matcha*, *sencha* and *genmaicha*. You can watch the *matcha* being whisked up at the counter.

Local Life
A Night on the Town

While the area around Ponto-chō and Kiyamachi-dōri may be swarming with tourists at night, this is still very much an area favoured by locals for an evening out – from drinking in hidden-away bars and dining at classic *kaiseki* restaurants to hanging out on the banks of the Kamo-gawa and hitting the hottest club.

....

1 Tsukimochiya Naomasa

Start off with a stroll down Ponto-chō (p46) and, when it comes to an end, the next stop is to head to this quaint old sweets shop on Kiyamachi-dōri. Make sure you arrive before it closes at 6pm to pick out one of the tasty desserts. Hold on to this as your after-dinner treat to enjoy by the Kamo-gawa.

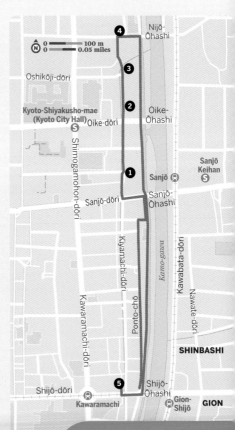

2 Tadg's Gastro Pub

Further along, the pretty stretch of Kiyamachi-dōri begins and there's no better place to take in the scenery than over a Japanese craft beer at **Tadg's Gastro Pub** (ダイグ ガストロ パブ; ☎075-213-0214; http://tadgs. com; 1st fl, 498 Kamikoriki-chō, Nakagyō-ku; drinks from around ¥500; ⏰11am-11pm; 🛜; ⓢTōzai line to Kyoto-Shiyakusho-mae), which attracts a mix of locals and expats. While the comfort pub food might be tempting, hold off for a special dinner nearby.

3 Kiyamachi Sakuragawa

A few steps from Tadg's, **Kiyamachi Sakuragawa** (木屋町 櫻川; ☎075-255-4477; Kiyamachi-dōri, Nijō-sagaru, Nakagyō-ku; lunch/dinner sets from ¥5000/10,000; ⏰11.30am-2pm & 5-9pm, closed Sun; ⓢTōzai line to Kyoto-Shiyakusho-mae) is a classic, refined *kaiseki* restaurant. The service is warm and welcoming, and the cuisine is delicious and comes presented like a piece of art.

4 Bar K6

For a post-dinner drink, continue dinner's elegant and sophisticated atmosphere with a tipple at **Bar K6** (バーK 6; ☎075-255-5009; 2nd fl, Le Valls Bldg, Nijō-dōri, Kiyamachi higashi-iru, Nakagyō-ku; drinks from ¥800; ⏰6pm-3am, to 5am Fri & Sat; ⓢTōzai line to Kyoto-Shiyakusho-mae, ⓡKeihan line to Jingu-Marutamachi) close by. Locals frequent this bar hidden on the 2nd floor at the far end of Kiyamachi-dōri for sensational cocktails and high-end whiskies. After a few, you might be feeling like a stretch of the legs and to walk off dinner and those drinks.

5 World

Make your way along the banks of the Kamo-gawa, where you can stroll along the riverside path, stopping for a rest on the grass and to devour the dessert you've been hanging onto. Then head back to the start of Kiyamachi-dōri to continue the night into the morning, dancing up a storm with locals, tourists and expats at Kyoto's favourite club, **World** (ワールド; ☎075-213-4119; http://world-kyoto. com; Basement, Imagium Bldg, 97 Shin-chō, Nishikiyamachi, Shijō-agaru, Shimogyō-ku; admission ¥2000-3000, drinks from ¥600; ⏰8pm-late; ⓡHankyū line to Kawaramachi).

A **B** **C** **D**

1

◉ *Nijō-jō*

Senbon-dōri

Aburanokoji-dōri

Ogawa-dōri

Shinmachi-dōri

❌11

Shinsen'en

Ⓢ Nijō-jō-mae

2

Oike-dōri

Horikawa-dōri

NAKAGYŌ-KU

Kamaza-dōri

Shinmachi-dōri

Aneyakōji-dōri

Sanjō-dōri

Rokkaku-dōri

Koin-dōri

3

Takoyakushi-dōri

Nishikikōji-dōri

4

Ōmiya Ⓗ

Ⓗ
Shijō-
Ōmiya

Mibu-dōri

Omiya-dōri

Kuromon-dōri

Horikawa-dōri

Nishinotoin-dōri

Ⓔ
13

Bukkōji-dōri

Takatsuji-dōri

For reviews see

◉ Top Sights   p36
◉ Sights   p46
❌ Eating   p47
Ⓓ Drinking   p50
Ⓔ Entertainment   p52
Ⓢ Shopping   p52

▲
Ⓝ
0 _____ 200 m
0 _____ 0.1 miles

5

Koromonotana-dōri
Muromachi-dōri
Ryōgaemachi-dōri

Karasuma-dōri

Kurumayachō-dōri
Higashinotoin-dōri
Ainomachi-dōri
Sakaimachi-dōri

Nijō-dōri

E **F** **G** **H**

Shimogamohon-dōri

Nijō-Ōhashi

Nijō-Ōhashi

Kamo-gawa

4

20
21

Teramachi-dōri

5

17

1 Kyoto International Manga Museum

Ōshikōji-dōri

Karasuma-Oike

Oike-dōri

Aneyakōji-dōri

Yanaginobanba-dōri

Oike-Ōhashi

Kyoto-Shiyakusho-mae
(Kyoto City Hall)

Oike-Ōhashi

6

14

3

Museum of Kyoto

Sanjō-dōri

Tominokōji-dōri
Fuyachō-dōri

24

Sanjō-dōri

Sanjō-Ōhashi

10

18

Rokkaku-dōri

8

Ponto-chō

2

Ponto-chō

Takakura-dōri

Sakaimachi-dōri

15

Takoyakushi-dōri

27

Kiyamachi-dōri

19

16

12

Nishikikōji-dōri

9

Nishiki Market

26

Kawaramachi

Shijō-Ōhashi

Shijō-dōri

Karasuma

Shijō

25

Shijō-dōri

22

7

Ayakōji-dōri

Kawaramachi-dōri

Takase-gawa

Kawabata-dōri

23

Bukkōji-dōri

Yanaginobanba-dōri

Tominokōji-dōri
Fuyachō-dōri
Gokomachi-dōri

Miyagawachō-dōri

Takatsuji-dōri

Matsubara-dōri

Sights

Kyoto International Manga Museum

MUSEUM

1 ◎ Map p44, E2

Located in an old elementary school building, this museum is the perfect introduction to the art of manga (Japanese comics). It has 300,000 manga in its collection, 50,000 of which are on display in the Wall of Manga exhibit. While most of the manga and displays are in Japanese, the collection of translated works is growing. In addition to the galleries that show both the historical development of manga and original artwork done in manga style, there are beginners' workshops and portrait drawings on weekends. (京都国際マンガミュージアム;

◎ Local Life

Shunsai Tempura Arima

Tempura is one of Japan's most divine dishes, and **Shunsai Tempura Arima** (旬菜天ぷら 有馬; Map p44, E5; 📞075-344-0111; 572 Sannochō, Muromachi-dōri, Takatsuji-agaru, Simogyō-ku; lunch/dinner sets from ¥1000/4750; ⊘11.30am-2pm & 5.30-10.30pm, closed Thu; 🏛; ⑤Karasuma line to Shijō) is a great place to try it. This friendly downtown restaurant is a tiny family-run joint with a welcoming atmosphere. The English-language menus and set meals make ordering easy. It's on a corner with a small English sign.

---

www.kyotomm.jp/english; Karasuma-dōri, Oike-agaru, Nakagyō-ku; adult/child ¥800/100; ⊘10am-6pm, closed Wed; ⑤Karasuma or Tōzai lines to Karasuma-Oike)

Ponto-chō

AREA

2 ◎ Map p44, H3

There are few streets in Asia that rival this narrow pedestrian-only walkway for atmosphere. Not much to look at by day, the street comes alive at night, with wonderful lanterns, traditional wooden exteriors, and elegant Kyoto-ites disappearing into the doorways of elite old restaurants and bars. (先斗町; Ponto-chō, Nakagyō-ku; ⑤Tōzai line to Sanjo-Keihan or Kyoto-Shiyakusho-mae, 🚉Keihan line to Sanjo, Hankyū line to Kawaramachi)

Museum of Kyoto

MUSEUM

3 ◎ Map p44, F2

This museum is worth visiting if a special exhibition is on (the regular exhibits are not particularly interesting and don't have much in the way of English explanations). On the 1st floor, the Roji Tempō is a reconstruction of a typical merchant area in Kyoto during the Edo period (this section can be entered free; some of the shops sell souvenirs and serve local dishes). Check the *Kyoto Visitor's Guide* for upcoming special exhibitions. (京都文化博物館; 📞075-222-0888; www.bunpaku.or.jp; Takakura-dōri, Sanjō-agaru, Nakagyō-ku; ¥500, extra for special exhibitions; ⊘10am-7.30pm, closed Mon; ⑤Karasuma or Tōzai lines to Karasuma-Oike)

Hi no Tori (Phoenix) sculpture in Kyoto International Manga Museum

Eating

Café Bibliotec Hello!

CAFE ¥

 4 Map p44, F1

As the name suggests, books line the walls of this cool cafe located in a converted *machiya* (traditional Japanese townhouse) attracting a mix of locals and tourists. It's a great place to relax with a book or to tap away at your laptop over a coffee or light lunch. Look for the huge banana plants out the front. (カフェビブリオティック ハロー！; ☎075-231-8625; 650 Seimei-chō, Nijō-dōri, Yanaginobanba higashi-iru, Nakagyō-ku; meals from ¥1000, coffee ¥450; ⏰11.30am-midnight; 🛜📶; 🚇Tōzai line to Kyoto-Shiyakusho-mae)

Honke Owariya

SOBA ¥

 5 Map p44, E1

Set in an old sweets shop in a traditional Japanese building on a quiet downtown street, this is where locals come for excellent soba (buckwheat noodle) dishes. The highly recommended house speciality, *hourai soba* (¥2160), comes with a stack of five small plates of soba with a selection of toppings, including shiitake mushrooms, shrimp tempura, thin slices of omelette and sesame seeds. (本家尾 張屋; ☎075-231-3446; www.honke-owariya. co.jp; 322 Kurumaya-chō, Nijō, Nakagyō-ku; soba from ¥760; ⏰11am-7pm; 📶; 🚇Karasuma or Tōzai lines to Karasuma-Oike)

Local Life
Vegetarian Dining

Biotei (びお亭; Map p44, E3; ☏ 075-255-0086; 2nd fl, M&I Bldg, 28 Umetada-chō, Sanjō-dōri, Higashinotōin nishi-iru, Nakagyō-ku; lunch/dinner sets from ¥840/1300; ⏱ lunch 11.30am-2pm Sun-Fri, dinner 5-8.30pm Tue, Thu, Fri & Sat; 🖉📶; 🚇Tōzai or Karasuma lines to Karasuma-Oike) is a favourite of Kyoto vegetarians, serving daily sets of Japanese food with dishes such as deep-fried crumbed tofu and black seaweed salad with rice, miso and pickles. The seating is rather cramped but the food is excellent, beautifully presented and carefully made from quality ingredients.

If Biotei is full, try your luck at **mumokuteki cafe** (ムモクテキカフェ; Map p44, G3; ☏ 075-213-7733; www.mumokuteki.com; 2nd fl, Human Forum Bldg, 351 Iseya-chō, Gokomachi-dōri, Rokkaku-sagaru, Nakagyō-ku; meals from ¥1000; ⏱ 11.30am-10pm; 🖉📶; 🚇Hankyū line to Kawaramachi), a vegetarian cafe above a shop and a lifesaver for many Kyoto vegetarians. The food is tasty, varied and served in casual, homely surroundings. Try the tofu and avocado burger paired with a fresh vegetable juice. Most of it is vegan, but non-vegan options are clearly marked on the picture menu.

Yoshikawa   TEMPURA ¥¥¥

6 🍴 Map p44, G2

This is the place to go for delectable tempura. Attached to the Yoshikawa

ryokan, it offers table seating, but it's much more interesting to sit and eat around the small counter and observe the chefs at work. It's near Oike-dōri in a fine traditional Japanese-style building. Reservation is required for the tatami room; counter and table seating are unavailable on Sunday. (吉川; ☏ 075-221-5544; www.kyoto-yoshikawa.co.jp; 135 Matsushita-chō, Tominokōji, Oike-sagaru, Nakagyō-ku; lunch ¥3000-25,000, dinner ¥8000-25,000; ⏱ 11am-2pm & 5-8.30pm; 📶; 🚇Tōzai line to Karasuma-Oike or Kyoto-Shiyakusho-mae)

Roan Kikunoi   KAISEKI ¥¥¥

7 🍴 Map p44, H4

Roan Kikunoi is a fantastic place to experience the wonders of *kaiseki* (Japanese haute cuisine). It's a clean, intimate space located right downtown. The chef takes an experimental and creative approach to *kaiseki* and the results are a wonder for the eyes and palate. It's highly recommended. You can reserve through your hotel or ryokan. (露庵菊乃井; ☏ 075-361-5580; www.kikunoi.jp; 118 Saito-chō, Kiyamachi-dōri, Shijō-sagaru, Shimogyō-ku; lunch/dinner from ¥4000/13,000; ⏱ 11.30am-1.30pm & 5-8.30pm; 🖉📶; 🚇Hankyū line to Kawaramachi or Keihan line to Gion-Shijō)

Kyōgoku Kane-yo   JAPANESE ¥

8 🍴 Map p44, G3

This is a good place to try *unagi* (eel). You can choose to either sit downstairs with a nice view of the waterfall, or upstairs on the tatami. The *kane-yo donburi* (eel over rice; ¥1400) set is excellent value. Look for the barrels of live eels outside and the wooden facade. (京極かねよ; ☎075-221-0669; 456 Matsugaechō, Rokkaku, Shinkyōgoku higashi-iru, Nakagyō-ku; unagi over rice from ¥1400; ⏱11.30am-9pm; 📷; Ⓢ Tōzai line to Kyoto-Shiyakusho-mae)

Ippūdō   RAMEN ¥

9 Map p44, F4

There's a reason that there's usually a line outside this place at lunchtime: the ramen is fantastic and the bite-sized *gyōza* (dumplings) are to die for. The *gyōza* set meal (¥750 or ¥850 depending on your choice of ramen) is great value. It's on Nishikikōji-dōri, next to a post office and diagonally across from a Starbucks. (一風堂; ☎075-213-8800; Higashinotō-in, Nishikikōji higashi-iru, Nakagyō-ku; ramen ¥750-950; ⏱11am-2am; 📷; Ⓢ Karasuma line to Shijō)

Mishima-tei   JAPANESE ¥¥¥

10 Map p44, G3

Mishima-tei is a good place to sample sukiyaki as the quality of the meat is very high, which is hardly surprising when there is a butcher right downstairs. It's at the intersection of the Sanjō and Teramachi covered arcades. Note that you'll need your hotel to make a booking for you as it doesn't accept reservations without a Japanese telephone number. (三嶋亭; ☎075-221-0003; 405 Sakurano-chō, Teramachi-dōri, Sanjō-sagaru, Nakagyō-ku; sukiyaki lunch/dinner from ¥7130/13,670; ⏱11.30am-9pm; 📷; Ⓢ Tōzai line to Kyoto-Shiyakusho-mae)

Cafe Phalam   CAFE ¥

11 Map p44, A2

A short walk from Nijō-jō, this homely cafe is a great spot to lunch on mainly vegan and vegetarian homemade food, from veggie burgers with salad to vegan cakes. The excellent coffee served in large cups is made

---

☑ Top Tip

Cheap Eats

If you've never tried a *kaiten-zushi* (conveyor-belt sushi restaurant), don't miss **Musashi Sushi** (寿しのむさし; Map p44, H2; ☎075-222-0634; www.sushinomusashi.com; Kawaramachi-dōri, Sanjō-agaru, Nakagyō-ku; plates ¥146; ⏱11am-10pm; 📷; Ⓢ Tōzai line to Kyoto-Shiyakusho-mae, Ⓡ Keihan line to Sanjō – most dishes are a mere ¥146. Not the best sushi in the world, but it's cheap, reliable and fun. It's also easy to eat here: you just grab what you want off the conveyor belt. If you don't see what you want, there's also an English menu to order from. Musashi is just outside the entrance to the Sanjō covered arcade; look for the miniature sushi conveyor belt in the window.

from beans sourced from Africa and South America, and the kids will be happy with the selection of toys. Near Lawson convenience store. (カフェパラン; ☏075-496-4843; Shin Nijo Bldg, 24 Hokusei-chō, Nishinokyo, Nakagyō-ku; cakes/meals from ¥350/700; ☉9am-8pm Mon-Fri, to 7pm Sat & Sun; 📶🚻📱; Ⓢ Tōzai line to Nijō-jō-mae, 🚉 JR line to Nijō Station)

Nishiki Warai OKONOMIYAKI ¥

 12 Map p44, F3

Nishiki Warai is a great place to try *okonomiyaki* (savoury pancakes) in casual surroundings. It can get a little smoky, but it's a fun spot to eat. Your *okonomiyaki* will be served ready-made to the hotplate at your table. It's about 20m west of the west end of Nishiki Market; look for the English sign in the window. (錦わらい; ☏075-257-5966; www.nishikiwarai. com; 1st fl, Mizukōto Bldg, 597 Nishiuoya-chō, Nishikikōji-dōri, Takakura nishi-iru, Nakagyō-ku; okonomiyaki from ¥700; ☉11.30am-midnight; 📱; Ⓢ Karasuma line to Shijō, 🚉 Hankyū line to Karasuma)

Drinking

Bungalow CRAFT BEER

 13 Map p44, C4

Spread over two floors, Bungalow serves a great range of Japanese craft beer in a cool industrial space. The menu changes regularly but generally you'll find 10 beers on tap from all over Japan, from a Baird Brewery Scotch ale to a peach Weizen from Minoh. It also does excellent food, most of which is organic. (バンガロー; ☏075-256-8205; www.bungalow.jp; Shijō-dōri, Shimoji-ku, Nakagyō-ku; ☉3pm-2am Tue-Sat, noon-11pm Sun; 🚉 Ōmiya)

Sama Sama BAR

 14 Map p44, H2

Sama Sama is an Indonesian-owned bar that feels like a very comfortable cave somewhere near the Mediterranean. Scoot up to the counter or make yourself at home on the floor cushions and enjoy a wide variety of drinks paired with food, including Indonesian classics like nasi goreng (¥800). It's down an alley just north of Sanjō; look for the signboard. (サマサマ; ☏075-241-4100; 532-16 Kamiōsaka-chō, Kiyamachi, Sanjō-agaru, Nakagyō-ku; drinks from ¥600; ☉6pm-2am, closed Mon; Ⓢ Tōzai line to Kyoto-Shiyakusho-mae)

Weekenders Coffee Tominoko-ji COFFEE

 15 Map p44, F3

Weekenders is a standing-room only coffee bar tucked away at the back of a parking lot in downtown Kyoto. Sure, it's a strange location but it's where you'll find some of the city's best coffee being brewed by roaster-owner, Masahiro Kaneko. (ウィークエンダーズ コーヒー; ☏075-746-2206; www.weekenders

MAYURA BENIJARATTANAPAKEE/SHUTTERSTOCK ©

Okonomiyaki (savoury pancake; p148)

coffee.com; 560 Honeyana-chō, Nakagyo-ku; coffee from ¥430; ⏰7.30am-6pm, closed Wed; 🚆Hankyū line to Kawaramachi)

Atlantis BAR

16 🚇 Map p44, H3

This is one of the few bars on Ponto-chō that foreigners can walk into without a Japanese friend. It's a slick, trendy place that draws a fair smattering of Kyoto's beautiful people, and wannabe beautiful people. In summer you can sit outside on a platform looking over the Kamo-gawa. (アトランティス; 📞075-241-1621; 161 Matsumoto-chō, Ponto-chō-Shijō-agaru, Nakagyō-ku; ⏰6pm-2am, to 1am Sun; 🚆Hankyū line to Kawaramachi)

Sake Bar Yoramu BAR

17 🚇 Map p44, F1

Named for Yoramu, the Israeli sake expert who runs Sake Bar Yoramu, this bar is highly recommended for anyone after an education in sake. It's very small and can only accommodate a handful of people. Sake tasting sets start at around ¥1600 for a set of three. By day, it's a soba restaurant called Toru Soba. (酒バー よらむ; 📞075-213-1512; www.sakebar-yoramu.com; 35-1 Matsuya-chō, Nijō-dōri, Higashinotoin, higashi-iru, Nakagyō-ku; sake tasting sets from ¥1600; ⏰6pm-midnight Wed-Sat; 🚇Kara-suma or Tōzai lines to Karasuma-Oike)

Entertainment

Kamogawa Odori
DANCE

18 Map p44, H3

Geisha dances from 1 to 24 May at Ponto-chō Kaburen-jō Theatre in Ponto-chō. (鴨川をどり; ☎075-221-2025; Ponto-chō, Sanjō-sagaru, Nakagyō-ku; normal/special seat/special seat with tea ¥2300/4200/4800; ☻shows 12.30pm, 2.20pm & 4.10pm; Ⓢ Tōzai line to Kyoto-Shiyakusho-mae)

Shopping

Aritsugu
HOMEWARES

19 🔒 Map p44, G3

While you're in Nishiki Market, have a look at this store – it has some of the best kitchen knives in the world. Choose your knife – all-rounder, sushi, vegetable – and the staff will show you

☑ Top Tip

Imported Gourmet Goods

The well-known Sanjō-dōri gourmet supermarket **Meidi-ya** (明治屋; Map p44, H2; ☎075-221-7661; Sanjō-dōri, Kawaramachi higashi-iru, Nakagyō-ku; ☻10am-9pm; Ⓡ Keihan line to Sanjō) has a great selection of imported food, in case you're missing some of your favourite things from home. It also has an excellent selection of wine.

how to care for it before sharpening and boxing it up. You can also have your name engraved in English or Japanese. Knives start at around ¥10,000. (有次; ☎075-221-1091; 219 Kajiya-chō, Nishikikōji-dōri, Gokomachi nishi-iru, Nakagyō-ku; ☻9am-5.30pm; Ⓡ Hankyū line to Kawaramachi)

Zōhiko
ARTS & CRAFTS

20 🔒 Map p44, G1

Zōhiko is the best place in Kyoto to buy one of Japan's most beguiling art and craft forms: lacquerware. If you aren't familiar with just how beautiful these products can be, you owe it to yourself to make the pilgrimage to Zōhiko. You'll find a great selection of cups, bowls, trays and various kinds of boxes. (象彦; ☎075-229-6625; www.zohiko.co.jp; 719-1 Yohojimae-chō, Teramachi-dōri, Nijō-agaru, Nakagyō-ku; ☻10am-6pm; Ⓢ Tōzai line to Kyoto-Shiyakusho-mae)

Ippōdō Tea
TEA

21 🔒 Map p44, G1

This old-style tea shop sells some of the best Japanese tea in Kyoto, and you'll be given an English leaflet with prices and descriptions of each one. Its *matcha* makes an excellent and lightweight souvenir; 40g containers start at ¥500. Ippōdō is located north of the city hall, on Teramachi-dōri. It has an adjoining teahouse, Kaboku Tearoom (p41; last order 5.30pm). (一保堂茶舗; ☎075-211-3421; www.ippodo-tea.co.jp; Teramachi-dōri, Nijō-agaru,

Lacquerware

YASIRICHA/SHUTTERSTOCK ©

Washi (handmade paper; p152)

Nakagyō-ku; ⊙9am-6pm; ⑤Tōzai line to Kyoto-Shiyakusho-mae)

Takashimaya   DEPARTMENT STORE

22 🔒 Map p44, H4

The grande dame of Kyoto department stores, Takashimaya is almost a tourist attraction in its own right, from the riches of the basement food floor to the wonderful selection of lacquerware and ceramics on the 6th floor. And don't miss the kimono display. (高島屋; ☎075-221-8811; Shijō-Kawaramachi Kado, Shimogyō-ku; ⊙10am-8pm, restaurants to 9.30pm; 🚆Hankyū line to Kawaramachi)

Wagami no Mise   ARTS & CRAFTS

23 🔒 Map p44, F5

This place sells a fabulous variety of *washi* (Japanese handmade paper) for reasonable prices and is a great spot to pick up a gift or souvenir. Look for the Morita Japanese Paper Company sign on the wall out the front. (倭紙の店; ☎075-341-1419; 1st fl, Kajinoha Bldg, 298 Ōgisakaya-chō, Higashinotōin-dōri, Bukkōji-agaru, Shimogyō-ku; ⊙9.30am-5.30pm Mon-Fri, to 4.30pm Sat; ⑤Karasuma line to Shijō)

Maruzen   BOOKS

Kyoto's most beloved bookshop closed in 2005 and finally reopened after 10 years in 2015. Occupying two basement floors of the BAL department store (see **27** 🔒 Map p44, H3), this excellent bookshop has a massive range of English-language books across all subjects on basement level 2, plenty of titles on Kyoto and Japan, a great selection of Japanese literature, magazines from around the globe and travel guides. (丸善; Basement fl, BAL, 251 Yamazaki-chō, Kawaramachi-sanjo sagaru, Nakagyō-ku; ⊙11am-9pm; 🚆Hankyū line to Kawaramachi)

Kyoto Design House   ARTS & CRAFTS

24 🔒 Map p44, G2

The Tadao Ando–designed Nikawa building is the perfect home for this design store, which stocks arts and crafts mainly designed by local Kyoto artists melding traditional with modern design. From handmade ceramics and *ohako* candy boxes to beautiful cushions using silk from the Nishijin textile district, this is the best place to pick up great gifts and souvenirs. (📞 075-221-0200; www.kyoto-dh.com; 1F Nikawa Bldg, Tominokōji-dōri, 105 Fukanaga-chō, Nakagyō-ku; ⏰11am-8pm; 🚇Karasuma or Tōzai lines to Karasuma-Oike)

Tokyu Hands
DEPARTMENT STORE

25 🔒 Map p44, E4

While the Kyoto branch of Tokyu Hands doesn't have the selection of bigger branches in places like Tokyo, it's still well worth a browse for fans of gadgets and unique homewares. It's a good place for an interesting gift or souvenir, from Hario coffee equipment and lacquerware bento boxes to Lomography cameras, stationery and cosmetics. (東急ハンズ京都店; 📞 075-254-3109; http://kyoto.tokyu-hands.co.jp; Shijō-dōri, Karasuma higashi-iru, Shimogyō-ku; ⏰10am-10.30pm; 🚇Karasuma line to Shijō)

Tsujikura
ARTS & CRAFTS

26 🔒 Map p44, H4

Tsujikura is a small store stocking the beautiful *wagasa* (waxed-paper umbrellas) the company has been manufacturing since the 17th-century, which come in a mix of colours with traditional and modern design. It also has a small selection of Isamu Noguchi's famous Akari paper lamps. It's on the 7th floor of the same building as the tourist information office near the

Shijō and Kawaramachi intersection. (辻倉; 📞 075-221-4396; www.kyototsujikura.com; 7th fl, Tsujikura Bldg, Kawaramachi-dōri, Shijō-agaru higashi-gawa, Nakagyō-ku; ⏰11am-7pm, closed Wed; 🚇Hankyū line to Kawaramachi)

BAL
DEPARTMENT STORE

27 🔒 Map p44, H3

For all your high-end fashion needs, the chic and elegant BAL department store is the place to go. You'll find fashion by Helmut Lang and Diane von Furstenberg as well as botanical skincare from Neal's Yard, and the ever popular Muji. The two basement floors house the huge Maruzen bookstore. (バル; www.bal-bldg.com/kyoto; 251 Yamazaki-chō, Kawaramachi-sanjo sagaru, Nakagyō-ku; ⏰11am-8pm; 🚇Hankyū line to Kawaramachi)

🔍 Local Life
Kamiji Kakimoto

One of the best places to buy *washi* (Japanese handmade paper) in Kyoto is **Kamiji Kakimoto** (紙司柿本; Map p44, G1; 📞 075-211-3481; 54 Tokiwagi-chō, Teramachi-dōri, Nijō-agaru, Nakagyō-ku; ⏰9am-6pm; 🚇Keihan line to Jingū-Marutamachi). It's got unusual items such as *washi* computer printer paper and *washi* wallpaper, along with great letter-writing and wrapping paper. Look for the hanging white *noren* (curtains) out the front.

Explore

Gion & Southern Higashiyama

Southern Higashiyama, at the base of the Higashiyama (Eastern Mountains), is Kyoto's richest area for sightseeing. Thick with temples, shrines, museums and traditional shops, it's great to explore on foot, with some pedestrian-only walkways plus parks and expansive temple grounds. It's also home to the Gion entertainment district and some of the city's finest ryokan (traditional Japanese inns).

The Sights in a Day

☀ Start your Southern Higashi-yama neighbourhood exploring by heading to **Kiyomizu-dera** (p58), one of the city's top temples. Take your time discovering the huge complex and enjoying the views over the city before a stroll through the lanes of **Ninen-zaka and Sannen-zaka** (p69). Stop in at **Kasagi-ya** (p70) for tea and sweets before a visit to the lovely temple and gardens at **Kōdai-ji** (p67). Slurp back delicious noodles at **Omen Kodai-ji** (p70) for lunch.

☀ Spend the first part of your afternoon at the vast temple complex of **Chion-in** (p60), then head away from the crowds to peaceful **Shōren-in** (p66) to admire the small but exquisite garden and drink a cup of *matcha* (powdered green tea) before a leisurely walk though **Maruyama-kōen** (p66) to **Yasaka-jinja** (p66).

☾ Hopefully you've made a reservation well in advance for the city's pinnacle of *kaiseki* (Japanese haute cuisine) at **Kikunoi** (p69). Then, as evening sets in, you'll want to make your way to **Gion** (p62) to wander the lantern-lit streets, keeping your eyes peeled for a glimpse of a geisha. Round off the evening with a drink at the sophisticated **Gion Finlandia Bar** (p72).

 Top Sights

💗 **Best of Kyoto**

Getting There

🚆 **Train** The private Keihan line provides access to Southern Higashiyama. Get off at Gion-shijō or Shichijō stations and walk uphill (east).

🚌 **Bus** Kyoto City buses serve various stops in the district and are a good way to access Kiyomizu-dera.

S Subway The Tōzai subway line's Higashiyama Station offers easy access to the northern end of the district.

Top Sights
Kiyomizu-dera

Kiyomizu-dera (清水寺; admission ¥400) is one of the city's most popular temples. Built around a holy spring (*kiyomizu* means 'pure water'), the temple has attracted pilgrims since the 8th century AD. In addition to halls holding fine Buddhist images, the complex includes a Shintō shrine that is associated with matters of the heart – buy a prayer plaque here to assure success in romance.

Map p64, E5

☎075-551-1234

www.kiyomizudera.or.jp

1-294 Kiyomizu, Higashiyama-ku

◷6am-6pm, closing times vary seasonally

🚌Kyoto City bus 206 to Kiyōmizu-michi, 🚉Keihan line to Kiyomizu-Gojō

Background

This ancient temple was first built in 798, but the present buildings are reconstructions dating from 1633. As an affiliate of the Hossō school of Buddhism, which originated in Nara, it has successfully survived the many intrigues of local Kyoto schools of Buddhism through the centuries and is now one of the most famous landmarks of the city (the reason it can get very crowded during spring and autumn).

The Hondō (Main Hall)

The Hondō (Main Hall), which houses a Jūichimen (11-headed) Kannon figure, features a huge verandah that juts out over the hillside, supported by 139 15m-high wooden pillars. Just below this verandah is Otowa-no-taki spring, where visitors drink the sacred waters believed to bestow health and long life.

Jishu-jinja

After exiting the Hondō/verandah, up to your left you will find Jishu-jinja, where visitors try to ensure success in love by closing their eyes and walking about 18m between a pair of 'Love Stones'.

Tainai-meguri

Before you enter the actual temple precincts, visit one of the oddest sights in Japan: the Tainai-meguri. By entering the hall, you are figuratively entering the womb of Daizuigu Bosattsu, a female Bodhisattva who has the power to grant any human wish.

☑ **Top Tips**

▶ The Main Hall is undergoing renovations and may be covered, though there is still access for visitors.

▶ Check out the temple's excellent website for information, plus a how-to guide for praying here.

▶ During the cherry-blossom season, autumn-foliage season and the summer O-Bon season (Buddhist observance honouring ancestral spirits), Kiyomizu-dera holds evening 'light-ups', when the trees and buildings are illuminated.

✕ **Take a Break**

Fill up on sushi, tasty noodles or *unagi* (eel) at Sobadokoro Shibazaki (p70).

Rest your legs over a cup of *matcha* (powdered green tea) at Kasagi-ya (p70), a traditional teahouse.

Top Sights
Chion-in

A collection of soaring buildings and spacious courtyards, Chion-in (知恩院) serves as the headquarters of the Jōdo sect, the largest sect of Buddhism in Japan. It's the most popular pilgrimage temple in Kyoto and it's always a hive of religious activity. For visitors with a taste for the grand, this temple is sure to satisfy.

Map p64, E2

www.chion-in.or.jp

400 Rinka-chō, Higashiyama-ku

inner buildings & garden adult/child ¥500/250, grounds free

🕑9am-4.30pm

S Tōzai line to Higashiyama

The main gate at Chion-in

Background

Chion-in was established in 1234 on the site where Hōnen, one of the most famous figures in Japanese Buddhism, taught his brand of Buddhism (Jōdo, or Pure Land, Buddhism) and eventually fasted to death.

Temple Highlights

The oldest of the present buildings date from the 17th century. The two-storey San-mon temple gate is the largest in Japan. The immense main hall (Miei-dō Hall), which measures 35m wide and 45m long, houses an image of Hōnen and is connected with the Dai Hōjō hall by a 'nightingale' floor that squeaks as one walks over it. Miei-dō Hall is under restoration and closed to the public. It's expected to be finished in 2019.

Temple Bell

Chion-in's temple bell was cast in 1633. It is the largest temple bell in Japan. It's up a flight of steps at the southeastern corner of the temple precincts. The bell is rung by the temple's monks 108 times on New Year's Eve each year.

Gardens

Walk around the back of the main hall to see the temple's gardens. On the way, you'll pass a darkened hall with a small statue of Amida Buddha glowing eerily. It's a nice contrast to the splendour of the main hall.

☑ Top Tips

▶ Like most other popular sights in Kyoto, it's best to head here first thing in the morning or late in the afternoon to avoid the crowds.

▶ This is a huge temple complex so set aside at least a couple of hours to explore it all.

✘ Take a Break

Stroll through Maruyama-kōen and into the Ninen-zaka area to the lovely cafe **Rakushō** (洛匠; ☏075-561-6892; 516 Washio-chō, Kodaijikitamon-dōri, Shimogawara higashi-iru, Higashiyama-ku; tea from ¥600; ⏱9.30am-6pm, closed irregularly; ☐; ☐Kyoto City bus 204 to Higashiyama-Yasui).

Book in advance and team your visit with lunch at arguably one of the city's best restaurants, Kikunoi (p69).

Top Sights
Gion

Gion is the famous entertainment and geisha quarter on the eastern bank of the Kamo-gawa. While Gion's true origins were in teahouses catering to weary visitors to the nearby shrine Yasaka-jinja, by the mid-18th century the area was Kyoto's largest pleasure district.

祇園周辺

Map p64, C3

Higashiyama-ku

S Tōzai line to Sanjō, **R** Keihan line to Gion-Shijō

Maiko (apprentice geisha)

Take a Wander

The best way to experience Gion these days is with an evening stroll around the atmospheric streets, which are lined with 17th-century traditional restaurants and teahouses. Start off on the main street, **Hanami-kōji**, which runs north–south and bisects Shijō-dōri.

If you walk from Shijō-dōri along the northern section of Hanami-kōji and take your third left, you will find yourself on Shimbashi (sometimes called Shirakawa Minami-dōri), which is one of Kyoto's most beautiful streets, especially in the evening and during cherry-blossom season.

A bit further north lie **Shinmonzen-dōri** and **Furumonzen-dōri**, running east–west. Wander in either direction along these streets, which are packed with old houses, art galleries and shops specialising in antiques.

☑ Top Tips

▶ Evening is the best time to stroll around Gion, when the lanterns are all lit up and you have the best chance of glimpsing a geisha.

✗ Take a Break

Slurp down the signature udon noodles at Omen Kodai-ji (p70).

Drop in for a civilised drink in the stylish Gion Finlandia Bar (p72).

E

Chion-in

1 Shōren-in

HIGASHIYAMA-KU

9 Kōdai-ji

D

6 Kōdai-ji

P

10 Camellia Tea Experience

8 Ninen-zaka & 7 Sannen-zaka Area

Ninen-zaka

4 Maruyama-kōen

Ishibei-kōji

12

3 Yasaka-jinja

Higashi-ōji-dōri

S Higashiyama

Higashiyama

Sanjō-dōri

Higashiōji-dōri

Shinmonzen-dōri

Shimbashi-dōri

19

Hanami-kōji

Gion

16

Yasaka-dōri

C

Kiri-dōshi

Sanjō-dōri

Furumonzen-dōri

Tominagachō-dōri

11 20

15

Hanami-kōji

SHINBASHI

Shijō-dōri

Yamatoōji-dōri

Sanjō Keihan

S

Sanjō-Ōhashi

Shijō-Ōhashi

17 Gion-Shijō

Gion-Shijō

Ponto-chō

Kawabata-dōri

Miyagawachō-dōri

18

B

Sanjō

Sanjō-dōri

Kiyamachi-dōri

Kawaramachi

Tōkaido-sen

A

Shijō-dōri

Gokomachi-dōri

1

2

3

4

Kiyomizu-dera

Gojō-dōri

Shibutani-dōri

Sannen-zaka

Kiyomizu-michi

Chawan-zaka

Gojō-zaka

13 ✗

Higashiōji-dōri

For reviews see

◎ Top Sights	p58
◎ Sights	p66
✗ Eating	p69
◎ Drinking	p71
◎ Entertainment	p72
◎ Shopping	p73

500 m
0.3 miles

N

Higashiōji-dōri

Kyoto
National
Museum ◎ 5

Shichijō-dōri

14 ◎

Sanjūsangen-
dō Temple

2 ◎

Shiokōji-dōri

Higashiōji-dōri

Yamatooji-dōri

Syomen-dōri

Gojō-
Ōhashi

Ⓚ Kiyomizu-
Gojō

Gojō-dōri

Toiyamachi-dōri

Sayamachi-dōri

Kawabata-dōri

Kamo-
gawa

Ⓚ Shichijō

Shichijō-
Ōhashi

Shiokōji-
bashi

Gojō-dōri

Sights

Shōren-in
BUDDHIST TEMPLE

1 Map p64, E1

This temple is hard to miss, with its giant camphor trees growing just outside the walls. Fortunately, most tourists march right on past, heading to the area's more famous temples. That is their loss, because this intimate little sanctuary contains a superb landscape garden, which you can enjoy while drinking a cup of green tea (¥400, 9am to 4pm; ask at the reception office). (青蓮院; 69-1 Sanjōbō-chō, Awataguchi, Higashiyama-ku; ¥500; ⏰9am-5pm; ⒮Tōzai line to Higashiyama)

Sanjūsangen-dō Temple
BUDDHIST TEMPLE

2 Map p64, B8

This superb temple's name refers to the 33 *sanjūsan* (bays) between the pillars of this long, narrow building. The building houses 1001 wooden

---

☑ Top Tip
Geisha-Spotting
The 'sport' of geisha-spotting has gotten out of hand, with tourists sometimes blocking the women's paths in popular districts like Gion in order to get photos. Let them through; *maiko* and geisha are professionals – if you want to get close to them, support their arts and go to see them perform (p72).

---

statues of Kannon (the Buddhist goddess of mercy); the chief image, the 1000-armed Senjū-Kannon, was carved by the celebrated sculptor Tankei in 1254. It is flanked by 500 smaller Kannon images, neatly lined in rows. The visual effect is stunning, making this a must-see in Southern Higashiyama and a good starting point for exploration of the area. (三十三間堂; ☎075-561-0467; 657 Sanjūsangendōma wari-chō, Higashiyama-ku; adult/child ¥600/300; ⏰8am-5pm 1 Apr-15 Nov, 9am-4pm 16 Nov-31 Mar; ☒Kyoto City bus 206 or 208 to Sanjūsangen-dō-mae, ⒭Keihan line to Shichijō)

Yasaka-jinja
SHINTO SHRINE

3 Map p64, D3

This colourful and spacious shrine is considered the guardian shrine of the Gion entertainment district. It's a bustling place that is well worth a visit while exploring Southern Higashiyama; it can easily be paired with Maruyama-kōen, the park just up the hill. (八坂神社; ☎075-561-6155; www.yasaka-jinja.or.jp; 625 Gion-machi, Kita-gawa, Higashiyama-ku; admission free; ⏰24hr; ⒮Tōzai line to Higashiyama)

Maruyama-kōen
PARK

4 Map p64, D3

Maruyama-kōen is a favourite of locals and visitors alike. This park is the place to come to escape the bustle of the city centre and amble around gardens, ponds, souvenir shops and restaurants. Peaceful paths

Yasaka-jinja

meander through the trees, and carp glide through the waters of a small pond in the park's centre. (円山公園; Maruyama-chō, Higashiyama-ku; **S** Tōzai line to Higashiyama)

Kyoto National Museum

MUSEUM

 5 ⊙ Map p64, B7

The Kyoto National Museum is the city's premier art museum and plays host to the highest-level exhibitions in the city. It was founded in 1895 as an imperial repository for art and treasures from local temples and shrines. In the original **main hall** there are rooms with displays of over 1000 artworks, historical artefacts and handicrafts. The **Heisei Chishinkan**, designed by Taniguchi Yoshio and opened in 2014, is a brilliant modern counterpoint to the original building. (京都国立博物館; www.kyohaku. go.jp; 527 Chaya-machi, Higashiyama-ku; ¥520; ⊙9.30am-5pm, to 6pm during special exhibitions, to 8pm Fri, closed Mon; 📮Kyoto City bus 206 or 208 to Sanjūsangen-dō-mae, 📮Keihan line to Shichijō)

Kōdai-ji

BUDDHIST TEMPLE

6 ⊙ Map p64, D4

This exquisite temple was founded in 1605 by Kita-no-Mandokoro in memory of her late husband, Toyotomi Hideyoshi. The extensive grounds include gardens designed by

Understand

Geisha

No other aspect of Japanese culture is as misunderstood as the geisha. First – and let's get this out of the way – geisha are not prostitutes. Simply put, geisha are highly skilled entertainers who are paid to facilitate and enliven social occasions in Japan.

Kyoto is the capital of the geisha world. Confusingly, here they are not called geisha; rather, they are called *maiko* or *geiko*. A *maiko* is a girl between the ages of 15 and 20 who is in the process of training to become a fully fledged *geiko* (the Kyoto word for geisha). During this five-year period, she lives in an *okiya* (geisha house) and studies traditional Japanese arts, including dance, singing, tea ceremony and *shamisen* (three-stringed instrument resembling a lute or a banjo). During this time she will start to entertain clients, usually in the company of a *geiko*, who acts like an older sister.

Due to the extensive training she receives, a *maiko* or *geiko* is like a living museum of Japanese traditional culture. In addition to her skills, the kimono she wears and the ornaments in her hair and on her obi (kimono sash) represent the highest achievements in Japanese arts.

While young girls may have been sold into this world in times gone by, these days girls make the choice themselves. The proprietor of the *okiya* will meet the girl and her parents to determine if the girl is serious and if her parents are willing to grant her permission to enter the world of the geisha.

It's easy to spot the difference between a *maiko* and a *geiko* – *geiko* wear wigs with minimal ornamentation (usually just a wooden comb), while *maiko* wear their own hair in an elaborate hairstyle with many bright hair ornaments called *kanzashi*. Also, *maiko* wear an elaborate long-sleeved kimono, while *geiko* wear a simpler kimono with shorter sleeves.

the famed landscape architect Kobori Enshū, and teahouses designed by the renowned master of the tea ceremony, Sen no Rikyū. The temple holds three annual special night-time illuminations, when the gardens are lit by multicoloured spotlights. The illuminations are held from mid-March to early May, 1 to 18 August and late October to early December. (高台寺; ☎075-561-9966; www.kodaiji.com; 526 Shimokawara-chō, Kōdai-ji, Higashiyama-ku; ¥600; ⏰9am-5.30pm; 🚌Kyoto City bus 206 to Yasui; Ⓢ Tōzai line to Higashiyama)

Ninen-zaka & Sannen-zaka Area
AREA

7 ◎ Map p64, D4

Just downhill from and slightly to the north of Kiyomizu-dera, you will find one of Kyoto's loveliest restored neighbourhoods, the Ninen-zaka–Sannen-zaka area. The name refers to the two main streets of the area: Ninen-zaka and Sannen-zaka, literally 'Two-Year Hill' and 'Three-Year Hill' (the years referring to the ancient imperial years when they were first laid out). These two charming streets are lined with old wooden houses, traditional shops and restaurants. (二年坂・三年坂; Higashiyama-ku; 🚌Kyoto City bus 206 to Kiyomizu-michi or Gojō-zaka; 🚃Keihan line to Kiyomizu-Gojō)

Camellia Tea Experience
TEA CEREMONY

8 ◎ Map p64, D4

Camellia is a superb place to try a simple Japanese tea ceremony. It's located in a beautiful old Japanese house just off Ninen-zaka. The host speaks fluent English and explains the ceremony simply and clearly, while managing to perform an elegant ceremony. The price includes a bowl of *matcha* and a sweet. The website has an excellent map and explanation. (茶道体験カメリア; ☎075-525-3238; www.tea-kyoto.com; 349 Masuya-chō, Higashiyama-ku; per person ¥2000; 🚌Kyoto City bus 206 to Yasui)

Eating

Kikunoi
KAISEKI ¥¥¥

9 ✕ Map p64, D3

This is one of Kyoto's true culinary temples, serving some of the finest *kaiseki* (Japanese haute cuisine) in the city by famous Michelin-starred chef Mutara. Located in a hidden nook near Maruyama-kōen, this restaurant has everything necessary for the full over-the-top *kaiseki* experience, from setting to service to exquisitely executed cuisine, often with a creative twist. Make a reservation through your hotel or ryokan concierge. (菊乃井; ☎075-561-0015; www.kikunoi.jp; 459 Shimokawara-chō, Yasakatoriimae-sagaru, Shimokawara-dōri,

Higashiyama-ku; lunch/dinner from
¥8000/15,000; ⏱noon-1pm & 5-8pm;
🚗 📶; 🚃Keihan line to Gion-Shijō)

Omen Kodai-ji
NOODLES ¥

10 Map p64, D4

Housed in a remodelled Japanese
building with a light, airy feeling, this
branch of Kyoto's famed Omen noodle
chain is the best place to stop while
exploring the Southern Higashiyama
district. The signature udon (thick,
white wheat noodles) served in broth
with a selection of fresh vegetables is
delicious, and there are many other à
la carte offerings. (おめん 高台寺店;
📞075-541-5007; 358 Masuya-chō, Kōdaiji-
dōri, Shimokawara higashi-iru, Higashiyama-
ku; noodles from ¥1150, set menu ¥1850;
⏱11am-9pm; 🚃Kyoto City bus 206 to
Higashiyama-Yasui)

 Local Life

Kasagi-ya

At **Kasagi-ya** (かさぎ屋; Map p64,
D4; 📞075-561-9562; 349 Masuya chō,
Kōdai-ji, Higashiyama-ku; tea & sweets
from ¥600; ⏱11am-6pm, closed Tue;
📶; 🚃Kyoto City bus 206 to Higashiyama-Yasui), on Sannen-zaka near
Kiyomizu-dera, you can enjoy a
nice cup of *matcha* and a variety
of sweets. This funky old wooden
shop has atmosphere to boot and
friendly staff – which makes it
worth the wait if there's a queue.
It's hard to spot – you may have to
ask one of the local shop owners.

Kagizen Yoshifusa
TEAHOUSE ¥

11 🍵 Map p64, C3

This Gion institution is one of Kyoto's
oldest and best-known *okashi-ya*
(sweet shops). It sells a variety of
traditional sweets and has a lovely
tearoom out the back where you
can sample cold *kuzukiri* (transpar-
ent arrowroot noodles) served with
a *kuro-mitsu* (sweet black sugar)
dipping sauce, or just a nice cup
of *matcha* and a sweet. (鍵善良房;
📞075-561-1818; www.kagizen.co.jp; 264 Gion
machi, Kita-gawa, Higashiyama-ku; kuzukiri
¥900; ⏱9.30am-6pm, closed Mon; 📶;
🚃Hankyū line to Kawaramachi, Keihan line
to Gion-Shijō)

Hisago
NOODLES ¥

12 🍴 Map p64, D4

If you need a quick meal while in the
main Southern Higashiyama sightseeing district, this simple noodle and
rice restaurant is a good bet. It's within
easy walking distance of Kiyomizu-dera
and Maruyama-kōen. *Oyako-donburi*
(chicken and egg over rice; ¥1010)
is the speciality of the house. (ひさ
ご; 📞075-561-2109; 484 Shimokawara-chō,
Higashiyama-ku; meals from ¥950; ⏱11.30am-
7.30pm, closed Mon; 📶; 🚃Kyoto City bus 206
to Higashiyama-Yasui)

Sobadokoro Shibazaki
NOODLES ¥

13 🍴 Map p64, C5

This spacious comfortable restaurant
is a great spot to fuel up while sight-

Chicken and rice dish

seeing in the Kiyomizu-dera area, and has something to please everyone. Fill up on *kaiten-sushi* (conveyor-belt sushi) on the ground floor or head upstairs for excellent soba noodles and well-presented tempura sets and *unagi* (eel) dishes. While you're upstairs, check out the sublime collection of Japanese lacquerware. (そば処柴崎; ☎075-525-3600; www. kyoto-shibazaki.com; 4-190-3 Kiyomizu, Higashiyama-ku; sushi per piece from ¥120, soba from ¥950; ⏰11am-9pm; 📷; 🚌Kyoto City bus 206 to Kiyomizu-michi, 🚃Keihan line to Kiyomizu-Gojō)

Drinking

Tōzan Bar
BAR

14 🍸 Map p64, B7

Even if you're not spending the night at the Hyatt Regency, drop by the cool and cosy underground bar for a tipple or two. Kitted out by renowned design firm Super Potato, the dimly lit atmospheric space features interesting touches, such as old locks, wooden beams, an antique-book library space and a wall feature made from traditional wooden sweet moulds. (ハイアットリージェンシー京都; ☎075-541-3201; www.kyoto.regency. hyatt.com; Hyatt Regency Kyoto, 644-2

Sanjūsangendō-mawari, Higashiyama-ku; ⏱5pm–midnight; 🚉Keihan line to Shichijō)

Gion Finlandia Bar

BAR

15 🍸 Map p64, C3

This stylish, minimalist Gion bar in an old geisha house is a great place for a civilised drink. There's no menu, so just prop up at the bar and let the bow-tied bartender know what you like, whether it's an expertly crafted cocktail or a high-end Japanese single malt. Friday and Saturday nights can get busy, so you may have to queue. (ぎおん フィンランディア バー; 📞075-541-3482; www.finlandiabar. com; 570-123 Gion-machi minamigawa,

---

🅠 Local Life

Beer Komachi

Located in the Furokawa-chō covered shopping arcade close to Higashiyama Station, **Beer Komachi** (ビア小町; Map p64, D1; 📞075-746-6152; www.beerkomachi. com; 444 Hachiken-chō, Higashiyama-ku; ⏱5-11pm Mon & Wed-Fri, 3-11pm Sat & Sun, closed Tue; 🛜; 🚇Tōzai line to Higashiyama) is a casual bar dedicated to promoting Japanese craft beer. There are usually seven Japanese beers on tap, which rotate on an almost-daily basis. The excellent bar-food menu tempts with delights such as fried chicken in beer batter and even a stout chocolate gateau for dessert.

Higashiyama-ku; cover ¥500, drinks around ¥1000; ⏱6pm–3am; 🚉Keihan line to Gion-Shijō)

Entertainment

Miyako Odori

DANCE

16 ⭐ Map p64, C3

This 45-minute dance is a wonderful geisha performance. It's a real stunner and the colourful images are mesmerising. It's held throughout April usually at the Gion Kōbu Kaburen-jō Theatre, on Hanami-kōji, just south of Shijō-dōri. As of late 2016, the building was under renovation and performances were held at Kyoto Art Theater Shunjuza in the meantime. (都をどり; 📞075-541-3391; www.miyako-odori. jp; Gionkobu Kaburenjo, 570-2 Gion-machi minamigawa, Higashiyama-ku; nonreserved seat/reserved seat/reserved seat with tea ¥2500/4200/4800; ⏱shows 12.30pm, 2pm, 3.30pm & 4.50pm; Kyoto City bus 206 to Gion, 🚉Keihan line to Gion-Shijō)

Minami-za

THEATRE

17 ⭐ Map p64, B3

The oldest kabuki theatre in Japan is the Minami-za in Gion. The major event of the year is the **Kaomise festival** (30 November to 25 December), which features Japan's finest kabuki actors. Other performances take place on an irregular basis – check the website for the schedule or with the Kyoto Tourist Information Center (p167). (南座; 📞075-561-0160; www.kabuki-bito.jp;

Shijō-Ōhashi, Higashiyama-ku; performances ¥5000-27,000; ®Keihan line to Gion-Shijō)

Kyō Odori DANCE

18 ⭐ Map p64, B4

Put on by the Miyagawa-chō geisha district, this wonderful geisha dance is among the most picturesque performances of the Kyoto year. It's held from the first to the third Sunday in April at the **Miyagawa-chō Kaburen-jō Theatre** (宮川町 歌舞練場), east of the Kamo-gawa between Shijō-dōri and Gojō-dōri. (京おどり; ☎075-561-1151; Miyagawachō Kaburenjo, 4-306 Miyagawasuji, Higashiyama-ku; nonreserved seat/nonreserved seat with tea/reserved seat/reserved seat with tea ¥2200/2800/4200/4800; ⊙shows 1pm, 2.45pm & 4.30pm; ®Keihan line to Gion-Shijō)

Shopping

Ichizawa Shinzaburo Hanpu FASHION & ACCESSORIES

19 🔒 Map p64, C1

This company has been making its canvas bags for over 110 years and the store is often crammed with those in the know picking up a skillfully crafted Kyoto product. Originally designed as 'tool' bags for workers to carry sake bottles, milk and ice blocks, the current designs still reflect this idea. Choose from a range of styles and colours. (一澤信三郎帆布; ☎075-541-0436; www.ichizawa.co.jp; 602

Kyō Odori performance

Takabatake-chō, Higashiyama-ku; ⊙9am-6pm; ⑤Tōzai line to Higashiyama)

Yojiya COSMETICS

20 🔒 Map p64, C3

Peruse the cosmetics and skincare here at one of Kyoto's most well-known brands. The famous oil-blotting facial papers make a great lightweight and cheap souvenir. There are a few branches around town – this one is on the corner of Shijō-dōri and Hanami-kōji; look for the logo of a face. (よーじや; ☎075-541-0177; Shijō-dōri, Higashiyama-ku; ⊙10am-8pm; ®Keihan line to Gion-Shijō)

SANKEI/GETTY IMAGES ©

Explore

Northern Higashiyama

This area is packed with first-rate attractions and soothing greenery, making it one of the best parts of the city for relaxed sightseeing. The main area stretches from Nanzen-ji in the south to Ginkaku-ji in the north, two temples linked by the lovely Path of Philosophy (Tetsugaku-no-Michi). Other attractions include Hōnen-in, a quiet temple overlooked by the crowds, and the superb Eikan-dō temple with city views.

JAVEN/SHUTTERSTOCK ©

The Sights in a Day

☀ Spend your morning exploring the beautiful, scenic temple complex and gardens at **Nanzen-ji** (p76), ducking into subtemples and shrines along the way. Next, make your way to **Konchi-in** (p85) to admire its stunning Crane and Tortoise garden before heading over to the impressive **Eikan-dō** (p82); be sure to climb up the pagoda for city views. Make a pit stop at **Hinode Udon** (p88) to fuel up for the afternoon.

☀ Swap temple-hopping for art museums over at the **Okazaki-kōen area** (p82), where you'll find the **Kyoto Municipal Museum of Art** (p85) and the **National Museum of Modern Art** (p85). Check out the nearby **Kyoto Handicraft Center** (p89) for excellent souvenirs and gifts, from books on culture to samurai swords.

☾ Head over to start your stroll along the famous **Path of Philosophy** (p82), a very picturesque canal lined with cherry-blossom trees. Detour to the lovely **Hōnen-in** (p82) temple and garden, then hop back on the path and visit **Ginkaku-ji** (p78). Once you've explored the Silver Pavilion, end the day with dinner at **Omen** (p85) nearby.

 Top Sights

Nanzen-ji (p76)

Ginkaku-ji (p78)

💜 **Best of Kyoto**

Eating
Omen (p85)

Goya (p86)

Falafel Garden (p86)

Shopping
Kyoto Handicraft Center (p89)

Tōzandō (p89)

Getting There

🚃 **Train** The Keihan line stops at stations on the west side of the district.

🚌 **Bus** Kyoto City bus 5 traverses the district. Several other city buses stop here as well.

S **Subway** The Tōzai subway line is the best way to access Northern Higashiyama.

Top Sights
Nanzen-ji

Nanzen-ji (南禅寺), a complex of Zen temples and subtemples tucked against the Higashiyama (Eastern Mountains), is the Platonic form of Japanese Buddhist temple. It's got it all: a fine little *kare-sansui* (dry landscape) garden, soaring main halls, great gardens and an incredibly scenic location.

Map p80, E7

http://nanzenji.com

86 Fukuchi-chō, Nanzen-ji, Sakyō-ku

Grounds free

⏱8.40am-5pm Mar-Nov, to 4.30pm Dec-Feb

🚌Kyoto City bus 5 to Eikandō-michi, Ⓢ Tōzai line to Keage

Background

Nanzen-ji began its life as a retirement villa for Emperor Kameyama. Upon his passing in 1291, it was dedicated as a Zen temple. It operates now as the headquarters of the Rinzai school of Zen.

Highlights

At the entrance to the temple stands the **San-mon gate** (1628; admission ¥500), its ceiling adorned with Tosa- and Kanō-school murals of birds and angels. Beyond the San-mon is the **Honden** (Main Hall) with a dragon painting on the ceiling.

Beyond the Honden, the **Hōjō** hall contains the Leaping Tiger Garden, a classical *kare-sansui* garden (admission ¥500). Sadly, a tape loop in Japanese detracts from the experience of the garden.

After visiting the Honden and the Leaping Tiger Garden, walk under the aqueduct and take a hard left and walk up the hill. Climb the steps to **Kōtoku-an**, a fine subtemple nestled at the base of the mountains. It's free to enter and you will have the place to yourself about half the time.

Despite its popularity it doesn't feel crowded, even during the autumn-foliage season (November), when the maples turn crimson and stand in beautiful contrast to the moss beneath their boughs.

☑ **Top Tips**

▶ While you're in the Hōjō, you can enjoy a cup of tea while gazing at a small waterfall (¥500; ask at the reception desk of the Hōjō).

▶ There are several lovely subtemples that surround the complex, including Nanzen-in, Konchi-in (p85) and Tenju-an, so it's worth exploring the area.

✕ **Take a Break**

Grab a drink at the casual Kick Up (p88) bar across the street from the Westin Miyako.

Take a short walk from the temple and past Eikan-dō for some lunchtime noodles at Hinode Udon (p88).

SUPERJOSEPH/SHUTTERSTOCK ©

Top Sights
Ginkaku-ji

At the northern end of the Path of Philosophy, Kyoto's famed Silver Pavilion is an enclosed paradise of ponds, thick moss, classical Japanese architecture and swaying bamboo groves. It is unquestionably one of the most luxurious gardens in the city and belongs near the top of any Kyoto sightseeing itinerary.

銀閣寺

Map p80, E2

2 Ginkaku-ji-chō, Sakyō-ku

adult/child ¥500/300

⏰8.30am-5pm Mar-Nov, 9am-4.30pm Dec-Feb

🚌Kyoto City bus 5 to Ginkakuji-michi stop

Background

In 1482 shogun Ashikaga Yoshimasa constructed a villa at this fine mountainside location, which he used as a genteel retreat from the turmoil of civil war. Although Ginkaku-ji translates as Silver Pavilion, this is simply a nickname to distinguish it from Kinkaku-ji (the Golden Pavilion on the other side of town).

The main hall, which overlooks the pond, was originally covered in black lacquer. After Yoshimasa's death it was converted to a temple. The temple belongs to the Shōkoku-ji sect of the Rinzai school of Zen.

The Gardens

You will find walkways leading through the gardens, which were laid out by painter and garden designer Sōami. The gardens include meticulously raked cones of white sand known as *kōgetsudai*, designed to reflect moonlight and enhance the beauty of the garden at night.

☑ Top Tips

▶ Visit when the crowds are likely to be thin: early on a weekday morning or just before closing.

▶ A rainy day is a lovely time to visit: the moss here is superb under a light rain.

✕ Take a Break

Stop in for a break at Omen (p85) for fantastic noodles in an elegant traditional Japanese house.

For reviews see

Shishi-gatani

Ginkaku-ji

Hōnen-in 2

Path of Philosophy
(Tetsugaku-no-Michi) 3

11

Shirakawa-dōri

Ginkaku-ji-Michi

Kaguraoka-dōri

Shinnyo-dō

SAKYŌ-KU

12

Imadegawa-dōri

Kyoto University

Yoshidahigashi-dōri

Mikage-dōri

Higashiōji-dōri

Konoe-dōri

13

Nanzen-ji 5
Oku-no-in

Eikan-dō 1

Biwa-ko Sosui Canal

Nanzen-ji

16

Shira-kawa

Kurodani Pagoda 10

Shira-kawa

Konchi-in 9

17 Keage

Shirakawa-dōri

HIGASHIYAMA-KU

Sanjō-dōri

0   0.25 miles
0   500 m

Nijō-dori

Kyoto Municipal Zoo

Heian Jingū 4

Okazaki-kōen

Kyoto Municipal Museum of Art 8

National Museum of Modern Art 7

15

Marutamachi-dōri

19
20

Higashitakeyachō-dōri

Higashiōji-dōri

Reisen-dōri

Nijō-dōri

Fureai-Kan Kyoto Museum of Traditional Crafts 6

Niōmon-dōri

18   14

Higashiyama

Sanjō-dōri

Higashiōji-dōri

Hanami-kōji

Shinmonzen-dōri

Shinbashi-dōri

Sights

Eikan-dō
BUDDHIST TEMPLE

1 Map p80, E6

Perhaps Kyoto's most famous (and most crowded) autumn-foliage destination, Eikan-dō is a superb temple just a short walk south of the famous Path of Philosophy. Eikan-dō is made interesting by its varied architecture, its gardens and its works of art. It was founded as Zenrin-ji in 855 by the priest Shinshō, but the name was changed to Eikan-dō in the 11th century to honour the philanthropic priest Eikan. (永観堂; ☏075-761-0007; www.eikando.or.jp; 48 Eikandō-chō, Sakyō-ku; adult/child ¥1000/400; ⊙9am-5pm; ☐Kyoto City bus 5 to Eikandō-michi, ⑤Tōzai line to Keage)

Hōnen-in
BUDDHIST TEMPLE

2 Map p80, E3

One of Kyoto's hidden pleasures, this temple was founded in 1680 to honour the priest Hōnen. It's a lovely, secluded temple with carefully raked gardens set back in the woods. The temple buildings include a small gallery where frequent exhibitions featuring local and international artists are held. If you need to escape the crowds that positively plague nearby Ginkaku-ji, come to this serene refuge. (法然院; 30 Goshonodan-chō, Shishigatani, Sakyō-ku; admission free; ⊙6am-4pm; ☐Kyoto City bus 5 to Ginkakuji-michi)

Path of Philosophy (Tetsugaku-no-Michi)
AREA

3 Map p80, E3

The Tetsugaku-no-Michi is one of the most pleasant walks in all of Kyoto. Lined with a great variety of flowering plants, bushes and trees, it is a corridor of colour throughout most of the year. Follow the traffic-free route along a canal lined with cherry trees that come into spectacular bloom in early April. It only takes 30 minutes to do the walk, which starts at Nyakuōji-bashi, above Eikan-dō, and leads to Ginkaku-ji. (哲学の道; Sakyō-ku; ☐Kyoto City bus 5 to Eikandō-michi or Ginkakuji-michi, ⑤Tōzai line to Keage)

Heian-jingū
SHINTO SHRINE

4 Map p80, B6

One of Kyoto's more popular sights, this shrine was built in 1895 to commemorate the 1100th anniversary of the founding of Kyoto. The shrine buildings are colourful replicas, reduced to a two-thirds scale, of the Imperial Court Palace of the Heian

Top Tip
Rainy-Day Sightseeing

Okazaki-kōen (Map p80, B6) is an expanse of parks and canals that lies between Niōmon-dōri and Heian-jingū. Two of Kyoto's significant museums are here – the National Museum of Modern Art (p85) and Kyoto Municipal Museum of Art (p85) – as well as two smaller museums. If you find yourself in Kyoto on a rainy day, there's enough indoor sightseeing to keep you dry.

BLANSCAPE/SHUTTERSTOCK ©

Eikan-dō

period (794–1185). About 500m in front of the shrine is a massive steel *torii* (shrine gate). Although it appears to be entirely separate, this is actually considered the main entrance to the shrine itself. (平安神宮; Nishitennō-chō, Okazaki, Sakyō-ku; garden adult/child ¥600/300; ⏰6am-5pm Nov-Feb, 6am-6pm Mar-Oct, garden 8.30am-4.30pm; §Tōzai line to Higashiyama)

Nanzen-ji Oku-no-in
BUDDHIST SHRINE

5 ◎ Map p80, E7

Perhaps the best part of Nanzen-ji is overlooked by most visitors: Nanzen-ji Oku-no-in, a small shrine hidden in a forested hollow behind the main precinct. It's here that pilgrims pray while standing under the falls, sometimes in the dead of winter. (南禅寺奥の院; Fukuchi-chō, Nanzen-ji, Sakyō-ku; admission free; ⏰dawn-dusk; 🚌Kyoto City bus 5 to Eikandō-michi, §Tōzai line to Keage)

Fureai-Kan Kyoto Museum of Traditional Crafts
MUSEUM

6 ◎ Map p80, B6

Well worth a visit for anyone interested in traditional Kyoto arts and crafts, Fureai-Kan has excellent exhibits on display, including woodblock prints, lacquerware, bamboo goods and gold-leaf work, with information panels in English. It's located in the basement of Miyako Messe (Kyoto International

Understand

Temples & Shrines

Is it a Temple or a Shrine?
The easiest way to tell them apart is to check the gate. The main entrance of a shrine is a *torii* – usually two upright pillars joined at the top by two horizontal crossbars and often painted bright vermilion. In contrast, the *mon* (main entrance gate) of a temple is constructed of several pillars or casements, joined at the top by a multitiered roof.

Dress Code
Unlike at some other temples around the world, there's no strict dress code as such for temples and shrines in Japan. But it still pays to be respectful. One thing to note is that in most sights you will be required to take off your shoes before entering the temple.

What to Do at a Shrine
If you want to do as the locals do, here is the basic drill: rinse your mouth and hands with pure water at a *temizuya* (small pavilion), using the stone ablution *chōzuya* (basin) and *hishaku* (bamboo ladle) provided for this purpose. Rinse both hands before pouring water into a cupped hand to rinse the mouth. Do not spit the water into the basin; rather, spit it onto the gravel that surrounds the basin.

Next, proceed to the *haiden* (worshippers' hall), which stands before the main hall of the shrine. Here, you will find an offering box over which a bell hangs with a long rope attached. Visitors toss a coin into the box, then grab and shake the rope to 'wake the gods', bow twice, clap loudly twice, bow again twice (once deeply, once lightly), and then step back and to the side.

What to do at a Temple
There are no steadfast rituals you must follow when visiting a Buddhist temple. At many temples, you can pay a small fee for a cup of *matcha* (powdered green tea) and a Japanese sweet, which you can enjoy while looking at the garden.

Exhibition Hall). (みやこめっせ・京都伝統産業ふれあい館; 9-1 Seishōji-chō, Okazaki, Sakyō-ku; admission free; ⏰9am-5pm, closed 18 & 19 Aug, 29 Dec-3 Jan; Ⓢ Tōzai line to Higashiyama)

National Museum of Modern Art
MUSEUM

7 ◉ Map p80, B6

This museum is renowned for its Japanese ceramics and paintings. There is an excellent permanent collection, which includes many pottery pieces by Kawai Kanjirō. The coffee shop here is a nice place for a break and overlooks a picturesque canal. The museum also hosts regular special exhibitions, so check the website for what's on. (京都国立近代美術館; www.momak.go.jp; Enshōji-chō, Okazaki, Sakyō-ku; ¥430, extra for special exhibitions; ⏰9.30am-5pm, to 8pm Fri Apr-Sep, closed Mon; Ⓢ Tōzai line to Higashiyama)

Kyoto Municipal Museum of Art
MUSEUM

8 ◉ Map p80, B6

This fine museum holds several major exhibitions a year, as well as a variety of free shows. It's always worth stopping by to see if something is on while you are in town. The pond behind the museum is a great place for a picnic. (京都市美術館; 124 Enshōji-chō, Okazaki, Sakyō-ku; admission varies; ⏰9am-5pm, closed Mon; Ⓢ Tōzai line to Higashiyama)

Konchi-in
BUDDHIST TEMPLE

9 ◉ Map p80, D7

Just southwest of the main precincts of Nanzen-ji, this fine subtemple has a wonderful garden designed by Kobori Enshū, known as the Crane and Tortoise garden. If you want to find a good example of the *shakkei* (borrowed scenery) technique, look no further. (金地院; 86-12 Fukuchi-chō, Nanzen-ji, Sakyō-ku; adult/child ¥400/200; ⏰8.30am-5pm Mar-Nov, to 4.30pm Dec-Feb; 🚌Kyoto City bus 5 to Eikandō-michi, Ⓢ Tōzai line to Keage)

Kurodani Pagoda
BUDDHIST PAGODA

10 ◉ Map p80, D5

This pagoda, which stands above the temple of Kurodani, offers one of the best views over the city. You cannot enter the pagoda itself, but you can climb to its base. Follow the steps that start about 150m southeast of the main hall of the temple. (金戒光明寺; 121 Kurodani-chō, Sakyō-ku; admission free; ⏰9am-4pm; 🚌Kyoto City bus 100 to Okazaki-michi)

Eating

Omen
NOODLES ¥

11 🍴 Map p80, E3

This elegant noodle shop is named after the thick white noodles that are served in broth with a selection of seven fresh vegetables. Just say *omen* and you'll be given your choice of hot or cold noodles, a bowl of soup to dip them in and a plate of vegetables (put these into the soup along with sesame seeds). (おめん; ☎075-771-8994; www.omen.co.jp; 74 Jōdo-ji Ishibashi-chō, Sakyō-ku; noodles from ¥1150; ⊙11am-9pm; 🅿; 🚌Kyoto City bus 5 to Ginkakuji-michi)

Goya

OKINAWAN ¥

12 Map p80, C2

This Okinawan-style restaurant has tasty food (with plenty of vegetarian options), a stylish interior and comfortable upstairs seating. It's perfect for lunch while exploring Northern Higashiyama and it's just a short walk from Ginkaku-ji. At lunch it serves simple dishes such as taco rice (¥880) and *gōya champurū* (bitter melon

stir-fry; ¥680), while dinners comprise a wide range of *izakaya* (Japanese pub) fare. (ゴーヤ; ☎075-752-1158; 114-6 Nishida-chō, Jōdo-ji, Sakyō-ku; meals from ¥680; ⊙11.30am-3.30pm & 5.30pm-midnight, closed Wed; 🅿🔌; 🚌Kyoto City bus 5 to Ginkakuji-michi)

Falafel Garden

ISRAELI ¥

13 Map p80, A1

If you're in need of a break from Japanese food, head to this casual spot near Demachiyanagi Station for excellent and filling falafel pita sandwiches or plates with generous dollops of homemade hummus, or a side of green chilli sauce for more of a kick. Set menus (from ¥1100) are great value. There's a small garden courtyard for sunny days. (ファラフェルガーデン; ☎075-712-1856; www.falafelgarden.com; 15-2 Kamiyanagi-chō, Tanaka, Sakyō-ku; falafel from ¥410; ⊙11am-9.30pm; 🅿🔌; 🚌Keihan line to Demachiyanagi)

Au Temps Perdu

FRENCH ¥

14 Map p80, B7

Overlooking the Shirakawa Canal, just across the street from the National Museum of Modern Art, this tiny indoor/outdoor French-style cafe is a lovely spot to take a break when sightseeing in the area. Check out the delicious cakes on display and pair them with a pot of tea, or spring for a light lunch along the lines of quiche and salad. (オ・タン・ペルデュ; ☎075-762-1299; 64 Enshōji-chō,

---

Local Life

Karako

Karako (からこ; Map p80, A6; ☎075-752-8234; 12-3 Tokusei-chō, Okazaki, Sakyō-ku; ramen from ¥650; ⊙11.30am-2pm & 5pm-midnight; 🔌; 🚌Kyoto City bus 206 to Higashiyama-Nijō) is a favourite ramen restaurant in Kyoto not far from the main Okazaki-kōen area. While there's not much on atmosphere, the ramen is excellent – the soup is thick and rich and the *chashū* (pork slices) melt in your mouth. The *kotteri* (thick soup) ramen is highly recommended. Look for the lantern outside.

Gyōza (dumplings)

Okazaki, Sakyō-ku; tea & cake set from ¥1100; ⏱11am-7pm, closed Mon; 🏠; 🚇Tōzai line to Higashiyama)

Kiraku OKONOMIYAKI ¥

15 Map p80, C7

This approachable and friendly *okonomiyaki* (savoury pancake) restaurant on Sanjō, close to Nanzen-ji and other popular Northern Higashiyama sights, is an excellent place to stop for lunch while exploring the area or for dinner after a long day of sightseeing. In addition to the usual *okonomiyaki* favourites, you'll find dishes such as *gyōza* (dumplings) and *yaki-soba* (soba noodle stir-fry). (きらく三条本店; 📞075-761-5780; 208 Nakanochō, Sanjō-Shirakawa, Higashiyama-ku; okonomiyaki from ¥700; ⏱11.30am-2pm & 5pm-midnight; 🏠; 🚇Tōzai line to Higashiyama or Keage)

Hinode Udon NOODLES ¥

16 Map p80, D5

Filling noodle and rice dishes are served at this pleasant shop with an English menu. Plain udon are only ¥500, but we recommend you spring for the *nabeyaki udon* (pot-baked udon in broth) for ¥950. This is a good lunch spot when temple-hopping in the Northern Higashiyama area. (日の出うどん; 📞075-751-9251; 36 Kitanobō-chō, Nanzenji, Sakyō-ku; noodles from ¥500; ⏱11am-3.30pm, closed Sun & occasionally Mon; 🏠; 🚌Kyoto City bus 5 to Eikandō-michi)

Drinking

Kick Up BAR

17 Map p80, D8

Located just across the street from the Westin Miyako Kyoto (ウェスティン都ホテル京都), this wonderful bar attracts a regular crowd of Kyoto expats, local Japanese and guests from the Westin. It's subdued, relaxing and friendly. (キックアップ; 📞075-761-5604; 331 Higashikomonoza-chō, Higashiyama-ku; drinks from ¥600; ⏱7pm-midnight, closed Wed; 🚇Tōzai line to Keage)

Entertainment

ROHM Theatre Kyoto THEATRE

18 Map p80, B7

The Kyoto Kaikan Theatre underwent a renovation early in 2016 and transformed into the ROHM Theatre Kyoto. Housed in a striking modernist building, it holds three multipurpose halls with a 2000-seater main hall hosting everything from international ballet and opera performances to comedy shows, music concerts and *nō* theatre. (京都観世会館; 📞075-771-6051; https://rohmtheatrekyoto.jp/english; 44 Okazaki Enshōji-chō, Sakyō-ku; tickets from ¥3000; ⏱box office 10am-7pm; 🚇Tōzai line to Higashiyama)

Shopping

Kyoto Handicraft Center

ARTS & CRAFTS

19 🔒 Map p80, B5

Split between two buildings, East and West, the Kyoto Handicraft Center sells a good range of Japanese arts and crafts, such as Hokusai woodblock prints (from ¥5000), Japanese dolls, pearls, clothing and a great selection of books on Japanese culture and travel guides. English-speaking staff are on hand and currency exchange is available. It's within walking distance of the main Higashiyama sightseeing route. (京都ハンディクラフトセンター; 📞075-761-7000; www.kyotohandicraftcenter. com; 17 Entomi-chō, Shōgoin, Sakyō-ku; ⏲10am-7pm; 🚌Kyoto City bus 206 to Kumano-jinja-mae)

Japanese doll

Tōzandō

GIFTS & SOUVENIRS

20 🔒 Map p80, B5

If you're a fan of Japanese swords and armour, you have to visit this wonderful shop on Marutamachi (diagonally opposite the Kyoto Handicraft Center). It has authentic swords, newly made Japanese armour, martial arts goods etc, and there's usually someone on hand who can speak English. (東山堂; 📞075-762-1341; 24 Shōgoin Entomi-chō, Sakyō-ku; ⏲10am-6pm; 🚌Kyoto City bus 206 to Kumano-jinja-mae)

Top Sights
Kinkaku-ji

Getting There

🚌 Kyoto City bus 205 from Kyoto Station to Kinkakuji-michi, Kyoto City bus 101 or 205 from Kyoto Station to Kinkakuji-mae

Kyoto's famed 'Golden Pavilion', Kinkaku-ji is one of the world's most impressive religious monuments. The image of the gold-plated pavilion rising over its reflecting pool is the kind that burns itself into your memory. But there's more to this temple than its shiny main hall. The grounds are spacious and include another pond, a tea arbour and some lovely greenery.

Background

Originally built in 1397 as a retirement villa for shogun Ashikaga Yoshi-mitsu, Kinkaku-ji was converted into a Buddhist temple by his son, in compliance with his wishes. Also known as Rokuon-ji, Kinkaku-ji belongs to the Shōkokuji school of Buddhism.

In 1950 a young monk consummated his obsession with the temple by burning it to the ground. The monk's story is fictionalised in Mishima Yukio's 1956 novel *The Temple of the Golden Pavilion*.

The Pavillion & Grounds

The three-storey pavilion is covered in bright gold leaf and features a bronze phoenix on top of the roof. The mirror-like reflection of the temple in the Kyō-ko pond is extremely photogenic, especially when the maples are ablaze in autumn.

In 1955 a full reconstruction was completed, following the original design exactly, but the gold-foil covering was extended to the lower floors.

After visiting the gold-plated pavilion, check out the Ryūmon-taki waterfall and Rigyo-seki stone, which looks like a carp attempting to swim up the falls. Nearby, there is a small gathering of stone Jizō figures onto which people throw coins and make wishes.

Sekka-tei Teahouse

The quaint teahouse Sekka-tei embodies the spirit of *wabi-sabi* (rustic simplicity) that defines the Japanese tea-ceremony ethic. It's at the top of the hill shortly before the exit of the temple.

金閣寺

1 Kinkakuji-chō, Kita-ku

¥400

⊘ 9am-5pm

☑ Top Tips

▶ Don't expect to have the place to yourself – Kinkaku-ji is on everyone's 'must-see' list. Try to visit early on a weekday morning.

▶ Another good time to visit is just before closing; the building glows in the sunset and makes for a great photo opportunity.

✘ Take a Break

There are a few eateries on the approach to the temple, as well as a small tea garden near the entrance that serves *matcha* (green powdered tea) and sweets.

Explore

Imperial Palace & Around

Kyoto's Imperial Palace neighbourhood is the greenest area in the city centre. Dominating the area are the grounds of the Imperial Palace and its park, while to the northwest sits Daitoku-ji – a world of Zen temples, lovely gardens and lanes. Head north, where the greenery continues at the Kyoto Botanical Gardens and the forest setting of the Shimogamo-jinja. This area is also home to Kyoto's traditional textile district, Nishijin.

The Sights in a Day

Jump on the subway and head out to the world of Zen temples at the **Daitoku-ji** (p100) complex. You'll need to dedicate the entire morning to exploring all of the subtemples here, with their impossibly sublime raked Zen gardens. Don't miss one of the best at **Kōtō-in** (p100), and be sure to allow time to sit and meditate here. For lunch head over to the cafe **Sarasa Nishijin** (p104), which is housed in an old *sento* (public bathhouse).

Once you've had lunch and wandered the surrounding streets checking out this local residential area and giving your meal time to digest, it's time to head to a real bathhouse for a relaxing soak at **Funaoka Onsen** (p104).

After testing out all the baths and the sauna there, make your way to the **Kyoto Imperial Palace Park** (p94) to wander the extensive grounds and take a self-guided tour of the **palace** (p96) buildings.

For a local's day in the Imperial Palace area, see p96.

 Top Sights

Kyoto Imperial Palace & Imperial Palace Park (p94)

Local Life

Parks, Tradition & Cafe Life (p96)

Best of Kyoto

Eating
Papa Jon's (p97)

Sarasa Nishijin (p104)

Getting There

S Subway Take the Karasuma line to access most of the sights, including the Imperial Palace Park and Daitoku-ji.

Bus Buses are the most convenient way to visit sights in the far north.

Top Sights
Kyoto Imperial Palace & Imperial Palace Park

The **Kyoto Imperial Palace** (京都御所; Kyoto Gosho, Nakagyō-ku; ⏱9am-5pm Apr-Aug, 9am-4.30pm Sep & Mar, 9am-4pm Oct-Feb, last entry 40min before closing, closed Mon) served as the official residence of the emperor of Japan from the late 12th century until the 19th century, and the palace remains an imperial household property. The original palace was built in 794 but suffered damage after being destroyed by fire numerous times; the current building dates to 1855.

Map p98, D7

www.kunaicho.go.jp

☎075-211-1215

admission free

Ⓢ Karasuma line to Marutamachi or Imadegawa

Jomei-mon gate, Kyoto Imperial Palace

These days the grand buildings no longer operate as the official residence of the Japanese emperor, though the palace and its surrounding park are the heart of Kyoto, both spatially and metaphorically. The palace recalls the city's proud heritage as the capital of the country and seat of the imperial court for over 1000 years.

The surrounding **Imperial Palace Park** (京都 御苑; Kyoto Gyōen, Nakagyō-ku; ☉dawn-dusk) occupies a huge expanse of central Kyoto – a green haven amid a sea of concrete. A wide variety of flowering trees are planted here and the plum arbor is a particularly pretty spot. This lovely park is where locals come for picnics and lazy strolls in the open fields. The Sentō Gosho (p101) is a second imperial property also located in the park and well worth a visit for its beautiful gardens.

☑ Top Tips

▶ If you plan on visiting the palace, wear comfortable shoes as the area is covered in large gravel stones that can make it tricky to walk on. The stones tend to get stuck in open sandals, too.

▶ The best time to visit the park is when it's most beautiful during cherry-blossom season (late March to early April).

✕ Take a Break

Stop in for a slice of authentic NYC cheesecake or a light lunch at Papa Jon's (p97), not far from the northern boundary of the park.

Local Life
Parks, Tradition & Cafe Life

The area around the Imperial Palace Park is where locals escape to when they need a bit of greenery in the city centre. Early morning joggers head to the park, families spend hours strolling through the Kyoto Botanical Gardens and people go about their daily routine at home in their *machiya* (traditional Japanese townhouses) in the textile district of Nishijin.

1 Imperial Palace Park

Kick off with a stroll around the ponds and palaces in the Imperial Palace Park (p94). You could rise early to join locals as they go for their morning jog; otherwise sleep in and go for a late morning wander instead. Stop in to check out the palace (p94) if you're interested in the Japanese imperial court.

❷ Nishijin

Wander west for a short while and you'll hit the traditional textile district of **Nishijin** (西陣; Nishijin, Kamigyō-ku; 🚌Kyoto City bus 9 to Horikawa-Imadegawa). This can be a lovely place to simply get lost in the backstreets, walking past *machiya* and witnessing the daily life of locals here.

❸ Nishijin Textile Center

While you're exploring the Nishijin area, stop by the **Nishijin Textile Center** (西陣織会館; 📞075-451-9231; www.nishijin ori.jp; Horikawa-dōri, Imadegawa-sagaru, Kamigyō-ku; ⏱10am-6pm; 🚌Kyoto City bus 9 to Horikawa-Imadegawa) to get a history lesson of the textile industry in this neighbourhood. You can see artisans at work during a weaving demonstration on the 2nd floor.

❹ Kyoto Botanical Gardens

If you have the stamina, go for a brisk walk (around 30 minutes) or head via subway back to Imadegawa Station and jump on the Karasuma line to Kitayama Station. From here you can head into the flower-filled **Botanical Gardens** (京都府立植物園; Shimogamohangi-chō, Sakyō-ku; gardens adult/child ¥200/free, greenhouse adult/child ¥200/free; ⏱9am-5pm, greenhouse 10am-4pm, closed 28 Dec-4 Jan; ⑤Karasuma line to Kitayama), where local families soak up the sun, and stop in at the greenhouse.

❺ Papa Jon's

Jump back on the subway to Imadegawa Station and make the short walk to end up at this **cafe** (パパジョンズカフェ 本店; 📞075-415-2655; 642-4 Shokokuji-chō, Karasuma-dōri, Kamidachiuri higashi-iru, Kamigyō-ku; lunch from ¥850; ⏱10am-9pm; 🈁🛜; ⑤Karasuma line to Imadegawa), a favourite of in-the-know locals for delicious cakes, light lunches and a welcoming atmosphere. Don't miss out on the excellent cheesecake.

❻ Demachi Futaba

You might have had your sugar fill at Papa Jon's, but don't let that stop you dropping by **Demachi Futaba** (出町ふたば; 📞075-231-1658; 236 Seiryucho, Imadegawa-agaru, Kawaramachi-dōri, Kamigyō-ku; sweets from ¥175; ⏱8.30am-5.30pm, closed Tue; 🚉Keihan line to Demachiyanagi). Get behind the queue of locals for the excellent sweets. Grab a few for later.

❼ Bon Bon Café

There's no better way to round out a day of walking and lazing in parks than with a drink. **Bon Bon Café** (ボンボンカフェ; 📞075-213-8686; http://madoi-co.com/restaurant/bon-boncafe; Kawaramachi, Imadegawa, Higashi-iru, Kitagawa, Kamigyō-ku; coffee/sandwiches from ¥400/700; ⏱11.30am-10pm, closed Mon; 🛜; 🚉Keihan line to Demachiyanagi) has a prime riverside position; you can pull up a chair outdoors on warmer days.

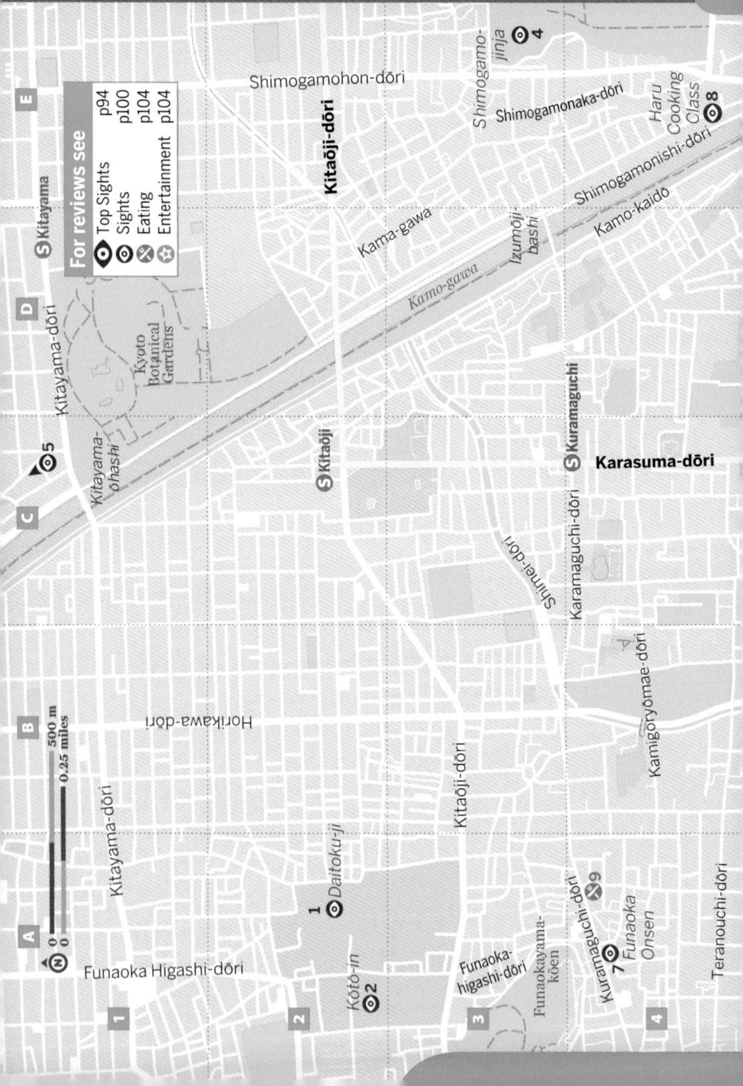

Shimogamohon-dōri

Shimogamo-Jinja ◉④

Shimogamonaka-dōri

Haru Cooking Class ◉⑧

Kitaōji-dōri

Shimogamonishi-dōri

Kamo-kaidō

Ⓢ Kitayama

Kitayama-dōri

Kama-gawa

Izumōji-bashi

Kamo-gawa

Kyoto Botanical Gardens

Ⓢ Kuramaguchi

Karasuma-dōri

Kitayama-ōhashi

Ⓢ Kitaōji

◉⑤

Karamaguchi-dōri

Shinmei-dōri

Horikawa-dōri

500 m
0.25 miles

Kitayama-dōri

Kitaōji-dōri

Kamigōryōmae-dōri

Daitoku-ji

Kuramaguchi-dōri

Kōto-in
◉②

①

Funaoka Onsen ⑦
✕⑨

Funaokayama-kōen

Teranouchi-dōri

Funaoka Higashi-dōri

Funaoka-higashi-dōri

Aoi-bashi

Kamo-Ōhashi

Kawaramachi-dōri

Kōjinguchi-dōri

Teramachi-dōri

Dōshisha University

Kyoto Imperial Palace Park

Kyoto Imperial Palace & Imperial Palace Park

3

Sentō Gosho Palace

Marutamachi-dōri

Karasuma- dōri

Imadegawa Ⓢ

Karasuma-dōri

Shinmachi-dōri

Marutamachi Ⓢ

✪10

Nakatachiuri-dōri

Nakachōjamachi-dōri

Takeyamachi-dōri

Kamitachiuri-dōri

Horikawa-dōri

Horikawa-dōri

Inokuma-dōri

Marutamachi- dōri

KAMIGYŌ-KU

◎6

Orinasu-kan

Imadegawa-dōri

Nakasuji-dōri

Motoseiganji-dōri

Yokoshinmei-dōri

Ichijō-dōri

Omiya-dōri

NISHIJIN

Sasayachō-dōri

Kamichōjamachi-dōri

Demizu-dōri

Jōfukuji-dōri

Uranomon-dōri

Shimotachiuri-dōri

Sawaragichō-dōri

Higurashi-dōri

Sights

Daitoku-ji
BUDDHIST TEMPLE

1 ◉ Map p98, A2

Daitoku-ji is a separate world within Kyoto – a world of Zen temples, perfectly raked gardens and wandering lanes. It's one of the most rewarding destinations in this part of the city, particularly for those with an interest in Japanese gardens. The eponymous Daitoku-ji temple (usually not open to the public) serves as the headquarters of the Rinzai Daitoku-ji school of Zen Buddhism. The highlights among the subtemples generally open to the public include Daisen-in, Kōtō-in, Ōbai-in, Ryōgen-in and Zuihō-in. (大徳寺; 53 Daitokuji-chō, Murasakino, Kita-ku; admission to subtemples varies; ⏱hours for subtemples varies; Ⓢ Karasuma line to Kitaōji)

Kōtō-in
BUDDHIST TEMPLE

2 ◉ Map p98, A2

On the far western edge of the Daitoku-ji complex, this sublime garden is one of the best in all Kyoto and it's worth a special trip. It's located within a fine bamboo grove that you traverse via a moss-lined path. Once inside there is a small stroll garden that leads to the centrepiece: a rectangle of moss and maple trees, backed by bamboo. Take some time on the verandah here to soak it all up. (高桐院; 73-1 Daitokuji-chō, Murasakino, Kita-ku; ¥400; ⏱9am-4.30pm; Ⓢ Karasuma line to Kitaōji)

Understand
Reservation & Admission to Kyoto's Imperial Properties

As of mid-2016, visitors no longer have to apply for permission to visit the Kyoto Imperial Palace. The palace is open to the public from Tuesday to Sunday and you just need to go straight to the main gate for entry. Children are permitted with an accompanying adult.

Permission to visit the Sentō Gosho and other imperial villas is granted by the Kunaichō, the Imperial Household Agency, which is inside the Imperial Palace Park. For morning tours, you have to fill out an application form and show your passport, or you can apply via its website. You must be over 18 years to enter each property. For afternoon tours, you can book tickets on the same day at the properties themselves from 11am. Only a certain number of tickets are issued each day, so it's first-come first-served. Sentō Gosho tours run for 60 minutes. All tours are free and are in Japanese with English audio guides available.

COWARDLION/SHUTTERSTOCK ©

Kōtō-in

Sentō Gosho Palace

HISTORIC BUILDING

3  Map p98, D7

The Sentō Gosho is the second imperial property located within the Kyoto Imperial Palace Park (the other one is the Imperial Palace itself). The structures are not particularly grand, but the gardens, laid out in 1630 by renowned landscape designer Kobori Enshū, are excellent. Tours (in Japanese) last for one hour. English audio guides are free of charge. You must be over 18 years old and you will need to bring your passport for ID. (仙洞御所; ☎075-211-1215; www.kunaicho. go.jp; Kyoto Gyōen, Nakagyō-ku; admission free; ⊙tours 9.30am, 11am, 1.30pm & 3pm; ⓢKarasuma line to Marutamachi or Imadegawa)

Shimogamo-jinja

SHINTO SHRINE

4  Map p98, E3

This shrine, dating from the 8th century, is a Unesco World Heritage site. It is nestled in the fork of the Kamo-gawa and Takano-gawa rivers, and is approached along a shady path through the lovely Tadasu-no-mori. This wooded area is said to be a place where lies cannot be concealed and is considered a prime location to sort out disputes. The trees here are mostly broadleaf (a rarity in

Understand

Religion

Shintō and Buddhism are the main religions in Japan. For much of history they were intertwined. Only about one-third of Japanese today identify as Buddhist, and the figure for Shintō is just 3%; however most Japanese participate in annual rituals rooted in both, which they see as integral parts of their culture and community ties. New Year's visits to shrines and temples are just one example. Generally in Japan, Shintō is concerned with this life: births and marriages for example are celebrated at shrines. Meanwhile, Buddhism deals with the afterlife: funerals and memorials take place at temples.

Shintō

Shintō, 'the way of the gods', is the indigenous religion of Japan. It locates divinity in the natural world. Its *kami* (gods) inhabit trees, rocks, waterfalls and mountains; however, they can also be summoned through rituals of dance and music into the shrines the Japanese have built for them, where they are beseeched with prayers for a good harvest, fertility and the like. The pantheon of deities includes thousands, from the celebrated sun goddess Amaterasu to the humble hearth *kami*.

Shintō has no central scripture, so it is hard to pin down, but one central tenet is purity. Visitors to shrines first wash their hands and mouth at a font at the gate; many rituals involve fire or water, prized for their cleansing powers. Over time, shrines have accrued specialisations – this one is good for business; that one for matchmaking.

Buddhism

When Buddhism entered Japan via Korea in the 6th century it didn't so much displace Shintō as envelop it; now there were *kami* and Bodhisattvas (beings who put off entry into nirvana in order to save the rest of us stuck in the corrupt world of time).

Several waves of Buddhist teachings arrived on Japanese shores, notably meditative Zen, Shingon (an esoteric sect related to Tantric Buddhism) and Pure Land, which taught of salvation in heaven (the Pure Land). It was the latter that most struck a chord with common Japanese, and Pure Land (called Jōdo-shū) remains the most popular form of Buddhism today. Kannon (the Bodhisattva of mercy and an important Pure Land figure) is the most worshipped deity in Japan.

Torii (shrine gate), Kamigamo-jinja

Kyoto) and they are gorgeous in the springtime. (下鴨神社; 59 Izumigawa-chō, Shimogamo, Sakyō-ku; admission free; 6.30am-5pm; 🚌Kyoto City bus 205 to Shimogamo-jinja-mae, 🚉Keihan line to Demachiyanagi)

Kamigamo-jinja
SHINTO SHRINE

5 ◎ Map p98, C1

Around 2km north of the Botanical Gardens is Kamigamo-jinja, one of Japan's oldest shrines, which predates the founding of Kyoto. Established in 679, it is dedicated to Raijin, the god of thunder, and is one of Kyoto's 17 Unesco World Heritage sites. The present buildings (more than 40 in all), including the impres-sive Haiden hall, are exact reproductions of the originals, dating from the 17th to 19th centuries. (上賀茂神社; ☎075-781-0011; www.kamigamojinja.jp; 339 Motoyama, Kamigamo, Kita-ku; admission free; ⊙6am-5pm; 🚌Kyoto City bus 9 to Kamigamo-misonobashi)

Orinasu-kan
MUSEUM

6 ◎ Map p98, A5

This atmospheric, and usually quiet, museum, housed in a Nishijin weaving factory, has impressive exhibits of Nishijin textiles. (織成舘; 693 Daikoku-chō, Kamigyō-ku; adult/child ¥500/350; 10am-4pm, closed Mon; 🚌Kyoto City bus No 9 to Horikawa-Imadegawa)

Funaoka Onsen

ONSEN

7 Map p98, A4

This old bath on Kuramaguchi-dōri is Kyoto's best. It boasts an outdoor bath, a sauna, a cypress-wood tub, an electric bath, a herbal bath and a few more for good measure. To get here, head west about 400m on Kuramaguchi-dōri from the Kuramaguchi and Horiikawa intersection. It's on the left, not far past Lawson convenience store. Look for the large rocks. (船岡温泉; https://funaokaonsen.info/en; 82-1 Minami-Funaoka-chō-Murasakino, Kita-ku; ¥430; ⏱3pm-1am Mon-Sat, 8am-1am Sun & holidays; 🚌Kyoto City Bus No 9 from Kyoto Station to Horikawa-Kuramaguchi)

Haru Cooking Class

COOKING

8 Map p98, E4

Haru Cooking Class is a friendly one-man cooking school located in a private home a little bit north of Demachiyanagi. The school's teacher, Taro, speaks English and can teach

both vegetarian (though fish stock may be used) and non-vegetarian cooking in classes that run for three to four hours. Reserve by email.

He also offers tours of Nishiki Market once a week at 12pm (per person ¥4000). (料理教室はる; http://www.kyoto-cooking-class.com/index.html; 166-32 Shimogamo Miyazaki-chō, Sakyō-ku; vegetarian/non-vegetarian per person from ¥5900/7900; ⏱classes from 2pm, reservation required)

Eating

Sarasa Nishijin

CAFE ¥

9 Map p98, A4

This is one of Kyoto's most interesting cafes – it's built inside an old *sentō* (public bathhouse) and the original tiles have been preserved. Light meals and coffee are the staples here. Service can be slow but it's worth a stop for the ambience. Lines out the door are not uncommon. It's near Funaoka Onsen. (さらさ西陣; ☎075-432-5075; 11-1 Murasakino Higashifujinomori-chō, Kita-ku; lunch from ¥960; ⏱noon-11pm, closed Wed; 🚌Kyoto City bus 206 to Daitoku-ji-mae)

Entertainment

Club Ōkitsu Kyoto

JAPANESE CULTURE

10 Map p98, C7

Ōkitsu provides an upmarket introduction to various aspects of Japanese cul-

✓ Top Tip

Cherry Blossoms Minus the Crowds

During cherry-blossom season (early April), the city's main tourist sites will be mobbed. If you want to enjoy the blossoms without the crowds, head to the banks of the Kamo-gawa or Takano-gawa, north of Imadegawa-dōri.

FRANK CARTER/GETTY IMAGES ©

Cherry-blossom trees in bloom

ture, including tea ceremony and the incense ceremony. The introduction is performed in an exquisite Japanese villa near the Kyoto Imperial Palace, and participants get a real sense of the elegance and refinement of traditional Japanese culture. (京都桜橘倶楽部「桜橘庵」; ☎075-411-8585; www.okitsu-kyoto.com; 524-1 Mototsuchimikado-chō, Kamichōjamachi-dōri, Shinmachi higashi-iru, Kamigyō-ku; Ⓢ Karasuma line to Imadegawa)

Local Life
Arashiyama

Getting There

🚃 JR Sagano/
San-in line from
Kyoto Station to
Saga-Arashiyama.

🚃 Keifuku Arashi-
yama, Randen, line
from Ōmiya Station to
Keifuku Arashiyama.

Arashiyama and Sagano is a tourist hotspot
thanks to its knockout scenery and a chance to
escape the city for some nature. That's exactly
why locals flock here at weekends – to wander its
temples spread out in the hills, stroll through the
bamboo grove, eat at top-rate restaurants and
take time out from hectic daily life.

❶ % Arabica

First stop is a good cup of coffee, and locals know that **% Arabica** (☎075-748-0057; www.arabica.coffee; 3-47 Susukinobaba-chō, Saga-Tenryūji, Ukyō-ku; ⏰8am-6pm; ⛶JR Sagano/San-in line to Saga-Arashiyama) is the place to get it. The shoebox-size cafe sits in a commanding place opposite the Hozu-gawa, with big glass windows looking out to the hills in the background. Grab a takeaway, admire the scenery and stroll along the river.

❷ Kameyama-kōen

Head upriver into the peaceful Kameyama-kōen, where locals come for some quiet and to hit the walking trails into the mountains. It's also a pretty spot to simply sit and relax. Occasionally monkeys spend time in the park looking for fruit from the trees, so keep your eyes peeled.

❸ Shigetsu

Once you've had your fill of relaxing in the park, it's time to fill up on lunch. Shigetsu is in the grounds of Tenryū-ji, and offers delicious and healthy Buddhist vegetarian cuisine, favoured by temple monks for centuries. Take in the garden views as you fuel up for the rest of your wander around the area.

❹ Arashiyama Bamboo Grove

It might be a tourist magnet but locals can't resist the ethereal beauty of the light peeking through the endless swaying bamboo stalks at the famous **Arashiyama Bamboo Grove** (嵐山竹林; Ogurayama, Saga, Ukyō-ku; admission free; ⏰dawn-dusk; ⛶Kyoto City bus 28 from Kyoto Station to Arashiyama-Tenryuji-mae, ⛶JR Sagano/San-in line to Saga-Arashiyama or Hankyū line to Arashiyama, change at Katsura). Try to get that perfect photo and spend some time admiring how visually stunning this spot is.

❺ Ōkōchi Sansō

As the Bamboo Grove comes to an end point you'll find the lavish estate, **Ōkōchi Sansō** (大河内山荘; 8 Tabuchiyama-chō, Sagaogurayama, Ukyō-ku; ¥1000; ⏰9am-5pm; ⛶Kyoto City bus 28 from Kyoto Station to Arashiyama-Tenryuji-mae, ⛶JR Sagano/San-in line to Saga-Arashiyama or Hankyū line to Arashiyama, change at Katsura), belonging to a famous samurai film actor. It's a beautiful place to wander through the stunning garden, which rises to views across to the mountains. There is also a lovely tearoom here where you can have a bowl of *matcha* and a sweet.

❻ Kitcho Arashiyama

Walk back through Kameyama-kōen towards the banks of the Hozu-gawa and take in the scenery as you stroll the riverside to your dinner destination. One of Kyoto's best *kaiseki* restaurants, Kitcho Arashiyama serves delicately prepared dishes in a private room with garden views.

Explore

Minami

Minami (ミナミ; 'south'), which includes the neighbourhoods Nam-ba, Shinsaibashi, Dōtombori and Amerika-Mura, is the funny man to Kita's straight man. It's here that you'll see the flashy neon signs and vibrant street life that you expect of Osaka. By day, Minami is primarily a shopping district; after dark, the restaurants, bars, clubs and theatres take over.

The Sights in a Day

☀ Grab breakfast and a coffee at the classic 1940s-style **Jun-kissa American** (p119). Afterwards, duck down a narrow laneway and pop your head into the temple **Hōzen-ji** (p116). Make your way over to the **Kuromon Ichiba** (p115) to peruse the goods on offer at this long-standing market and then head over to **Dōguya-suji Arcade** (p121) to stock up on every kitchen item imaginable. For lunch you can't go past the famous Osaka street-food snack of *tako-yaki* (octopus dumplings) at **Wanaka Honten** (p116).

⋯⋯⋯⋯⋯⋯⋯⋯⋯⋯⋯⋯⋯⋯⋯⋯

☀ In the afternoon, stroll through **Shinsaibashi-suji Shōtengai** (p122), detouring every now and then for a bit of book shopping and browsing at **Standard Books** (p121) and **Village Vanguard** (p122).

⋯⋯⋯⋯⋯⋯⋯⋯⋯⋯⋯⋯⋯⋯⋯⋯

☾ Make your way over to Ebisu-bashi before joining the nightly throngs in neon-lit **Dōtombori** (p110). There are plenty of places to eat here, such as **Imai Honten** (p117) and **Shoubentango-tei** (p117). Then walk over to **Amerika-Mura** (p115), which is full of bars and clubs.

For a local's day in Minami, see p112.

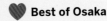

👁 **Top Sights**

Dōtombori (p110)

🔍 **Local Life**

Shin-Sekai (p112)

💜 **Best of Osaka**

Eating

Wanaka Honten (p116)

Chibō (p116)

Shoubentango-tei (p117)

Imai Honten (p117)

Drinking & Nightlife

Circus (p119)

Jun-kissa American (p119)

Misono Building (p120)

Folk Rock Bar Phoebe (p120)

⋯⋯⋯⋯⋯⋯⋯⋯⋯⋯⋯⋯⋯⋯⋯⋯

Getting There

S Subway Namba and Shinsaibashi subway stations, both on the Midō-suji line, are convenient for this area.

Top Sights
Dōtombori

Highly photogenic Dōtombori is the city's liveliest night spot. Its name comes from the 400-year-old canal, Dōtombori-gawa, now lined with walkways and a riot of illuminated billboards glittering off its waters. Just south and parallel to the canal is a pedestrianised street, where dozens of restaurants and theatres vie for attention with the flashiest of signage.

道頓堀

Map p114, C3

www.dotonbori.or.jp

S Midō-suji line to Namba, exit 14

Glico Running Man

Of all the illuminated signs along the canal, the one for Osaka-based candymaker Glico – a runner triumphantly crossing a finish line – is the most iconic. It first went up in 1935; the sign was last redone in 2014 and is now lit with low-energy LEDs instead of neon. The best view of the sign is from Ebisu-bashi (戎橋).

Kuidaore Tarō

Kuidaore Tarō, a drum-banging clown, is another Osaka icon, who represents the city's culture of *kuidaore* ('eat 'til you drop'). He made his first appearance in the 1950s. The most famous statue of him is at the entrance to the Nakaza Cuidaore Building (p116).

Kani Dōraku Honten

Dōtombori is full of eye-catching (and literal) shop signs – none more so than the giant animated crab that marks the entrance to **Kani Dōraku Honten** (かに道楽本店; 1-6-18 Dōtombori, Chūō-ku; S Midō-suji line to Namba, exit 14), which is, of course, a crab restaurant. Out front, the shop sells tasty crab sushi rolls (from ¥1200) to go.

Street Food

Dōtombori's pedestrian strip is lined with food vendors fronted by larger-than-life signs advertising *gyōza* (dumplings), *tako-yaki* (octopus dumplings) and more. Two of the most popular pit stops are Kinryū Ramen (p118), a noodle shop marked by a massive dragon (*ryū* means 'dragon'), and Daruma Dōtombori-ten (p118), which specialises in the deep-fried skewers called *kushikatsu* (look for the statue of the angry man holding skewers).

☑ Top Tips

▶ Signs are illuminated from 6pm to midnight, making this the most popular time to visit.

▶ Dōtombori's main strip often gets very crowded in the evening, no matter what day of the week (as most visitors are tourists). The **Tonbori River Walk**, the promenades on either side of the canal, are usually less hectic.

▶ Famous food vendors can draw long lines; waits are usually shorter during the day (and there are plenty of non-famous places to eat too).

▶ There are some benches for sitting and eating take-away.

✕ Take a Break

If you're in need of a quiet place to sit and eat, duck into noodle shop Imai Honten (p117).

Take a coffee break at Jun-kissa American (p119) on the Sennichi-mae *shōtengai* (market street), which runs perpendicular to Dōtombori's pedestrian street.

Local Life
Shin-Sekai

A century ago, Shin-Sekai ('new world') was home to a cutting-edge amusement park. Now this entertainment district mixes down-on-its-heels with retro cool. It's got ancient (and a little sketchy) *pachinko* (pinball-style game) and mahjong parlours, but also cheap and fun restaurants, a nostalgic mid-20th century atmosphere and a big bathing complex.

....

1 Shin-Sekai Ichiba
Okay, **Shin-Sekai Ichiba** (新世界市場), a covered shopping arcade, has seen better days, and many of the shopfronts here are shuttered. But some scrappy vendors remain, selling tea, traditional sweets and other sundry goods. In the last few years, an advertising giant has sponsored young artists to create posters for the shops, which hang in the arcade (and some are quite funny).

SHIN-SEKAI

Sakai-suji

Hanshin Expwy 14

Jyan-jyan-yokochō

Tennō-ji-kōen

S Dōbutsuen-mae

Abiko-suji

❷ Tsūten-kaku

Tsūten-kaku (通天閣; ☎06-6641-9555; www.tsutenkaku.co.jp; 1-18-6 Ebisu-higashi, Naniwa-ku; adult/student/child ¥700/500/300; ⏰9am-9pm; Ⓢ Midō-suji line to Dōbutsuen-mae, exit 5, Ⓡ JR Loop line to Shin-Imamiya) is the symbol of Shin-Sekai. When it was built in 1912 it was, at 63m, the second-tallest structure in Asia. Damaged by fire in 1943, it was rebuilt in 1956; the new steel-frame tower is 103m-high. As far as towers go, it's not impressive – it's the sentimental value that counts.

❸ Jyan-jyan-yokochō

Jyan-jyan-yokochō (ジャンジャン横丁) is named for the twang (*jyan*) of the *shamisen* (traditional three-stringed instrument), which could once be heard here. A century ago, this narrow lane connected Shin-Sekai to a since-disbanded red-light district. The cheap and lively restaurants, which still exist today, sprung up to tempt drunk patrons passing through.

❹ Spa World

Spa World (スパワールド; ☎06-6631-0001; www.spaworld.co.jp; 3-4-24 Ebisu-higashi, Naniwa-ku; 3hr/day pass Mon-Fri ¥2400/2700, Sat & Sun ¥2700/3000, additional ¥1300 midnight-5am; ⏰10am-8.45am; Ⓢ Midō-suji line to Dōbutsu-en-mae, exit 5, Ⓡ JR Loop line to Shin-Imamiya) has hot-spring baths inspired by locales around the world. It's good fun, and a good introduction to the Japanese cult of bathing (bathe in the buff, towels provided). There's also a waterpark area where swimsuits are worn and everyone hangs out together.

❺ Shin-Sekai Main Strip

Shin-Sekai's main strip is lined with restaurants clamouring for your attention. Smack in the middle is a giant pufferfish-shaped lantern advertising – you guessed it – a *fugu* (blowfish) restaurant. Speaking affectionately, locals describe this stretch as peak Osaka.

❻ Billiken

Walking through Shin-Sekai, there's no avoiding **Billiken**, a golden Kewpie doll–like character sitting on a pedestal reading 'The God of Things as they Ought to Be' in English. Designed by a Kansas City art teacher in the early 1900s, Billiken arrived in Osaka for the opening of the Tsūten-kaku – and has stuck around since.

❼ Daruma

Shin-Sekai's signature food is *kushikatsu* (skewers of meat, seafood and vegetables breaded and deep-fried). **Ganso Kushikatsu Daruma Honten** (元祖串かつ だるま本店; ☎06-6645-7056; www.kushikatu-daruma.com; 2-3-9 Ebisu-Higashi, Naniwa-ku; skewers ¥110-220; ⏰11am-10.30pm; ▣; Ⓢ Midōsuji line to Dōbutsuen-mae, exit 5), in business since 1929, is said to be the birthplace of the dish; there are several branches but, for many Japanese, a pilgrimage to the original shop is a necessary part of any visit to Osaka.

❽ Nocosare-jima

Cap off your visit with a stop by **Nocosare-jima** (のこされ島; www.nocoto.com; 2nd fl, 1-17-7 Ebisu-higashi, Naniwa-ku; ⏰7pm-1am; Ⓢ Midō-suji line to Dōbutsuen-mae, exit 5), a cosy, mellow bar with a beach shack vibe, and Southeast Asian and Okinawan munchies.

19

Hanshin Expwy

25
Crysta Underground Mall   Nagahori-dōri

Yotsubashi   Shinsaibashi   Unagidani-Kita-dōri
SHINMACHI   28   Unagidani-Minami-dōri

Nagahoribashi

NISHI-KU   **SHINSAIBASHI**   Daihōji-dōri   **CHŪŌ-KU**
9

18   Shimizu-dōri   **HIGASHI-**
15   14   13   26   **SHINSAIBASHI**

27   1 *Amerika-*   Suomachi-dōri
29   *Mura*   20
        AMERIKA-
        MURA   Hachiman-dōri
8   22   24   Mitsudera-dōri

17   Tombori River Walk

Dōtombori-   Tombori River Walk
gawa   Nakaza 4 12   **Dōtombori**
        Cuidaore 11 6   10
        Building 16
        7 3   **DŌTOMBORI**
Namba   Hōzen-ji   Nipponbashi
Namba
        Kintetsu   Kintetsu
JR Namba   Namba   Nipponbashi   *Kuromon*
                Ichiba
NAMBA   2
                Kuromon Ichiba

30   5   **URA-**
                NAMBA
        23   Nansan-dōri
NANIWA-KU

        Nankai
        Namba   **DENDEN**
                TOWN

For reviews see	

21

0   200 m
N 0   0.1 miles

Shoppers in Kuromon Ichiba

Sights

Amerika-Mura

AREA

1  Map p114, B2

West of Midō-suji, Amerika-Mura is a compact enclave of hip, youth-focused and offbeat shops, plus cafes, bars, tattoo and piercing parlours, night clubs, hair salons and a few discreet love hotels. In the middle is Triangle Park (p116), an all-concrete 'park' with benches for sitting and watching the fashion parade. Come night, it's a popular gathering spot. (アメリカ村, America Village, Ame-Mura; Nishi-Shinsaibashi, Chūō-ku; ⑤Midō-suji line to Shinsaibashi, exit 7)

Kuromon Ichiba

MARKET

2 Map p114, D4

An Osaka landmark for over a century, this 600m-long market is equal parts functioning market and tourist attraction. Vendors selling fresh fish, meat, produce and pickles attract chefs and local home cooks; shops offering takeaway sushi or with grills set up (to cook the steaks, oysters etc that they sell) cater to visitors – making the market excellent for grazing *and* photo-ops. (黒門市場, Kuromon Market; www.kuromon.com; Nipponbashi, Chūō-ku; ⏰most shops 10am-5pm, closed Sun; ⑤Sakai-suji line to Nipponbashi, exit 10)

Local Life
Triangle Park

In the middle of Ame-Mura is **Triangle Park** (三角公園, Sankaku-kōen; Map p114, B2; Nishi-Shinsaibashi, Chūō-ku; ⑤Midō-suji line to Shinsaibashi, exit 7), an all-concrete 'park' with benches for sitting and watching the fashion parade. Come night, it's a popular gathering spot.

Hōzen-ji
BUDDHIST TEMPLE

3 Map p114, C3

This tiny temple hidden down a narrow alley houses a statue of Fudō Myō-ō (a deity of esoteric Buddhism), covered in thick moss. It's a favourite of people employed in *mizu shōbai* ('water trade' – a euphemism for the sexually charged nightworld), who pause before work to throw some water on the statue. (法善寺; http://houzenji.jp; 1-2-16 Namba, Chūō-ku; ⑤Midō-suji line to Namba, exit 14)

Nakaza Cuidaore Building
NOTABLE BUILDING

4 Map p114, C3

Home of the most famous statue of Kuidaore Tarō – the drum-banging clown who represents the city's culture of *kuidaore* ('eat 'til you drop'). (中座くいだおれビル; 1-7-21 Dōtombori, Chūō-ku; ⑤Midō-suji line to Namba, exit 14)

Eating

Wanaka Honten
STREET FOOD ¥

5 Map p114, C4

This famous *tako-yaki* stand, just north of Dōguya-suji arcade, uses custom copper hotplates (instead of cast iron) to make dumplings that are crisper on the outside than usual (but still runny inside). There's a picture menu, and tables and chairs in the back. One popular dish to try is *tako-sen* (たこせん) – two dumplings sandwiched between *sembei* (rice crackers). (わなか本店; ☑06-6631-0127; http://takoyaki-wanaka.com; 11-19 Sennichi-mae, Chūō-ku; tako-yaki per 8 from ¥450; ⊙10am-10pm Mon-Fri, 8.30am-10pm Sat & Sun; ⑤Midō-suji line to Namba, exit 4)

Chibō
OKONOMIYAKI ¥¥

6 Map p114, C3

Chibō is one of Osaka's most famous *okonomiyaki* restaurants. It almost always has a line, but it moves fast because there is seating on multiple floors (though you might want to hold out for the coveted tables overlooking Dōtombori canal). Try the house special *Dōtombori yaki,* with pork, beef, squid, shrimp and cheese, and *tonpei-yaki* (omelette wrapped around fried food). (千房; ☑06-6212-2211; www.chibo.com; 1-5-5 Dōtombori, Chūō-ku; mains ¥885-1675; ⊙11am-1am Mon-Sat, to midnight Sun; 回; ⑤Midō-suji line to Namba, exit 14)

Shoubentango-tei   KAISEKI ¥¥¥

7 Map p114, C3

That this *kappō-ryōri* (Osaka-style haute cuisine) restaurant isn't more expensive is surprising considering its pedigree: established over 100 years ago, it was a literati hangout in the early 20th century. Even the cheapest course, which includes five dishes decided that day by the chef, tastes – and looks! – like a luxurious treat; reservations are necessary for all but the cheapest course. (正弁丹吾亭; ☎06-6211-3208; 1-7-12 Dōtombori, Chūō-ku; dinner course ¥3780-10,800; ⏱5-10pm; 📱; Ⓢ Midō-suji line to Namba, exit 14)

Imai Honten   UDON ¥¥

Step into an oasis of calm amid Dōtombori's chaos to be welcomed by kimono-clad staff at one of the area's oldest and most revered udon specialists. Try *kitsune udon* – noodles topped with soup-soaked slices of fried tofu. Look for the traditional exterior near Daiki Suisan (see 11 Map p114, C3), and the willow tree outside. (今井本店; ☎06-6211-0319; www.d-imai. com; 1-7-22 Dōtombori, Chūō-ku; dishes from ¥765; ⏱11am-10pm Thu-Tue; 😊📱; Ⓢ Midō-suji line to Namba, exit 14)

Za Ikaga   STREET FOOD ¥

8 Map p114, B2

The signature dish at this small food stand is *ika-yaki* – grilled squid, served here in a thin crêpe splattered with egg, mayonaise and savoury,

okonomiyaki-style sauce. There are a few seats inside at the counter and a few folding chairs on the street (perfect for watching the comings and goings in Amerika-Mura). There's a picture menu. (ザ・イカが; ☎06-6212-0147; www.ikayaki.jp; 2-12-8 Nishi-Shinsaibashi, Chūō-ku; dishes from ¥300; ⏱6pm-4am Thu-Tue; Ⓢ Midō-suji line to Shinsaibashi, exit 7)

Nishiya   JAPANESE ¥¥

9 Map p114, C2

A peaceful retreat from the busy streets of Shinsaibashi, this welcoming Osaka landmark serves udon noodles, hearty *nabe* (hot pot) dishes and *shabu-shabu* (thin slices of meat and vegetables cooked in a broth and dipped in sauce) for reasonable prices. Look for the traditional three-storey wooden building with sliding-door entrance, just north of the corner. (にし家; ☎06-6241-9221; www.nishiya. co.jp; 1-18-18 Higashi-Shinsaibashi, Chūō-ku; dishes & lunch sets ¥650-1700, dinner courses ¥3760-7540; ⏱11am-11pm Mon-Sat, to 9.30pm Sun; 😊📱; Ⓢ Midō-suji line to Shinsaibashi, exit 5 or 6)

Zauo   SEAFOOD ¥¥

10 Map p114, D3

Zauo has tables on long 'fishing boats' over tanks where patrons fish for their own dinner – particularly fun for kids, if they're not squeamish. If you hook something, there's celebratory drumming and your fish is whisked away to be prepared how you like (priced according to the type of fish). Dishes are meant for sharing. (ざうお難波本店; ☎06-6212-5882; www.zauo.com; Basement fl, Hotel Sunroute, Nipponbashi 1-1-13; dishes ¥680-3600; ☺5pm-midnight Mon-Fri, 11.30am-midnight Sat & Sun; 🖥♿; **S**Sakaisuji line to Nipponbashi, exit 6)

Kinryū Ramen
RAMEN ¥

Beneath the massive green dragon, this indoor-outdoor spot near Daiki Suisan (see 11 Map p114, C3) offers house-made noodles and a front-row seat to the Dōtombori scene. Purchase a ticket from a machine, sit at a low table on a tatami platform, top your noodle soup with *kimchi*, garlic or marinated green onion, and slurp away. The *chāshū* (sliced roast pork) ramen is particularly good. Don't linger too long, as there always seems to be a queue. (金龍ラーメン; ☎06-6211-6202; 1-7-26 Dōtombori, Chūo-ku; regular/chāshū ramen ¥600/900; ☺24hr; **S**Midō-suji line to Namba, exit 14)

Daiki Suisan
SUSHI ¥¥

11 Map p114, C3

This deceptively big *kaiten-sushi* restaurant, with over 50 seats, has a prime Dōtombori location. Plates are colour coded by price and thoughtfully labelled in multiple languages; staff speak some English too. Non-sushi-eaters can get cooked foods including *tori no karaage* (fried chicken) and fried tuna. (大起水産; ☎06-6214-1055; 1-7-24 Dōtombori, Chūo-ku; dishes ¥110-540; ☺11am-11pm; 🖥🖥; **S**Midō-suji line to Namba, exit 14)

Daruma Dōtombori-ten
KUSHIKATSU ¥¥

12 Map p114, C3

The Dōtombori branch of famous *kushikatsu* specialist Daruma (p113) can draw long lines (though there are plenty of seats, so it moves fast). Start with the 'Dōtombori set' of nine skewers and one appetiser for ¥1510. Look for the statue of the angry man holding skewers. (だるま 道頓堀店; ☎06-6213-8101; 1-6-4 Dōtombori, Chūo-ku; skewers ¥120-230; ☺11.30am-10.30pm; **S**Midō-suji line to Namba, exit 14)

Planet 3rd
CAFE ¥

13 Map p114, B2

This large, comfortable cafe in Ame-Mura serves good coffee, drinks and eclectic light meals, including pastas, sandwiches, salads and rice bowls. It's got a trendy decor with big windows for people-watching and a few iPads for guest use. (プラネットサード心斎橋店; 1-5-24 Nishi-Shinsaibashi, Chūo-ku; breakfast buffet ¥1080, lunch/dinner mains from ¥920; ☺7am-midnight; 🖥🛜; **S**Midō-suji line to Shinsaibashi, exit 7)

Banco
CAFE ¥

14 Map p114, B2

Opening onto a typically narrow Ame-Mura lane, artsy Banco serves good coffee (espresso ¥330), panini and *salumi*. Stop by for lunch or evening drinks. (バンコ; ☎080-6113-2504; 1-9-26 Nishi-Shinsaibashi, Chūo-ku; sandwiches from ¥550, lunch sets ¥1080; ☺11.30am-2am; 🖥; **S**Midō-suji line to Shinsaibashi, exit 7)

Kinryū Ramen restaurant

Drinking

Circus
CLUB

15 Map p114, B2

This small club is the heart of Osaka's underground electronic scene, drawing a crowd more for the music than a pick-up scene. The dance floor is nonsmoking. It's open on Friday and Saturday nights and sometimes during the week. Look up for the small sign in English and bring picture ID. (☎06-6241-3822; http://circus-osaka.com; 2nd fl, 1-8-16 Nishi-Shinsaibashi, Chūō-ku; ¥2000-2500; ⊘11pm-late; ⑤Midō-suji line to Shinsaibashi, exit 7)

Jun-kissa American
CAFE

16 Map p114, C3

With its 1940s interior intact and waitresses in long skirts, American is a classic *jun-kissa* – a shop from the first wave of cafes to open in Japan, during the post-WWII American Occupation. Come before 11am for a 'morning set' (¥620) of pillow-y buttered toast, a hard-boiled egg and coffee. Look for the chrome sign out front. (純喫茶アメリカン; ☎06-6211-2100; 1-7-4 Dōtombori, Chūō-ku; ⊘9am-11pm; ⑤Midō-suji line to Namba, exit 15)

Folk Rock Bar Phoebe
BAR

17 Map p114, B3

Crammed with vinyl and knick-knacks, Phoebe looks like a drinks counter operated out of an old hippie's storage closet (we mean that in a good way). The friendly owner spins folk-rock tunes on the record player, mixes good cocktails (from ¥700) and serves tasty food. There's an English sign out front. (108 Dōtombori Heights, 2-7-22 Nishi-Shinsaibashi, Chūō-ku; ☺7pm-2am; **S**Midō-suji line to Namba, exit 14)

Rock Rock
BAR

18 Map p114, B2

Serving the music-loving community since 1995, Rock Rock has a history of hosting after parties for international acts and attracting celeb visitors.

Local Life

Ura-Namba

Ura-Namba (literally 'behind Namba') is an unofficial district made up of clusters of small restaurants and bars in the shadow of Namba Nankai Station. It's becoming an increasingly trendy place to hang out. A good place to start is the **Misono Building** (味園ビル; Map p114, C4; 2nd fl, Misono Bldg, 2-3-9 Sennichi-mae, Chūō-ku; ☺6pm-late; **S**Sakai-suji line to Nipponbashi, exit 5), a once grand (and now wilting) structure, which has dozens of bars on the 2nd floor.

Regular events with a modest cover charge (usually ¥1500, including one drink ticket) showcase some of Osaka's finest rock DJs (and famous guests). (ロックロック; www.rockrock. co.jp; 3rd fl, Shinsaibashi Atrium Bldg, 1-8-1 Nishi-Shinsaibashi, Chūō-ku; ☺6pm-5am Mon-Sat, to 1am Sun; **S**Midō-suji line to Shinsaibashi, exit 7)

Mel Coffee Roasters
CAFE

19 Map p114, A1

This tiny takeaway stand – the vintage Probat roaster takes up half of it – raised the bar for coffee in Osaka when it opened in 2016. The owner speaks good English and will happily discuss the taste profiles of the various single-origin hand-pours on offer. (メル・コーヒー・ロースターズ; ☏06-4394-8177; www.mel-coffee. com; 1-20-4 Shinmachi, Nishi-ku; coffee from ¥400; ☺9am-7pm Tue-Fri, 11am-7pm Sat & Sun; **S**Yotsubashi line to Yotsubashi, exit 2)

Cinquecento
BAR

20 Map p114, D2

The name is Italian for '500', appropriate since everything at this small cocktail bar costs ¥500. It's not far from the corner of Sakai-suji; look for the 5 in a red circle. Things pick up later in the evening. (チンクエチェント; 2-1-10 Higashi-Shinsaibashi, Chūō-ku; ☺8pm-5am Mon-Sat, to 3am Sun; **S**Sakai-suji line to Nagahoribashi, exit 7)

Entertainment

Namba Bears   LIVE MUSIC

21 ⭐ Map p114, B5

For going on three decades this has been the place to hear underground music live in Osaka. It's a small, bare-concrete, smokey place – well suited to the punk, rock and indie bands that play here. In keeping with the alternative spirit, you can bring in your own beer. Most shows start at 7pm; tickets usually cost ¥2000 to ¥2500. (難波ベアーズ; ☑06-6649-5564; http://namba-bears.main.jp; 3-14-5 Namba-naka, Naniwa-ku; ⑤Midō-suji line to Namba, exit 4)

Hokage   LIVE MUSIC

22 ⭐ Map p114, B2

Looking like an office with the inner walls ripped out (which is entirely likely), Hokage is a fitting venue for the rock, punk and noise bands that play here. It's a small space, where the band might take up half the room. Downstairs is a lounge with tatty sofas that hums with the music from above. (火影; ☑06-6211-2855; www.musicbarhokage.net; Basement fl, 2-9-36 Nishi-Shinsaibashi, Chūō-ku; tickets around ¥1500; ⓧhours vary; ⑤Midō-suji line to Shinsaibashi, exit 7)

Shopping

Dōguya-suji Arcade   MARKET

23 Map p114, C4

This long arcade sells just about anything related to the preparation,

 Top Tip

Look Up, Look Down

When wandering the narrow streets of Osaka late at night, convinced that spot you're looking for must have closed or moved, remember that bars and pubs throughout Japan are often tucked away in the upper floors and basements of buildings. Check signs on the sides of buildings showing what's on each floor, and learn how to ask 'Where is...?' in Japanese (*...wa doko des ka?*).

consumption and selling of Osaka's principle passion: food. There's everything from bamboo steamers and lacquer miso soup bowls to shopfront lanterns and, of course, moulded hotplates for making *tako-yaki*. Hours vary per store. (道具屋筋; www.doguyasuji.or.jp/map_eng.html; Sennichi-mae, Chūō-ku; ⓧ10am-6pm; ⑤Midō-suji line to Namba, exit 4)

Standard Books   BOOKS

24 🔒 Map p114, B2

This cult-fave Osaka bookstore prides itself on not stocking any best sellers. Instead, it's stocked with small press finds, art books, indie comics and the like, plus CDs and quirky fashion items and accessories. (スタンダードブックストア; ☑06-6484-2239; www.standardbookstore.com; 2-2-12 Nishi-Shinsaibashi, Chūō-ku; ⓧ11am-10.30pm; ⑤Midō-suji line to Shinsaibashi, exit 7)

Tokyu Hands

DEPARTMENT STORE

25 🔒 Map p114, C1

Nominally a DIY and houseware chain, Tokyu Hands is Japan's favourite place to browse for items you probably didn't need but will end up loving. It's stacked floor-upon-floor with everything from obscure tools to design-forward lighting, clocks, curios and craft supplies, just for starters. There's a smaller branch in Umeda (p138). (東急ハンズ; www.tokyu-hands.co.jp; 3-4-12 Minami-Senba, Chūō-ku; 🕙10am-9pm; Ⓢ Midō-suji line to Shinsaibashi, exit 1)

Shinsaibashi-suji Shōtengai

SHOPPING CENTRE

26 🔒 Map p114, B2

East of Midō-suji, Shinsaibashi is one of Japan's great shopping zones, most notably in this eight-block-long covered arcade that's crammed with domestic and international clothing brands, drugstores, bookstores and other sundry retailers. On weekends it's estimated that the arcade attracts 100,000-plus shoppers, so expect crowds. (心斎橋筋商店街; www.shinsai-bashi.or.jp; Ⓢ Midō-suji line to Shinsaibashi, exit 4)

Flake Records

MUSIC

27 🔒 Map p114, A2

Flake is Osaka's most in-the-know music shop, selling new and used, local and import, CDs and records. The owner speaks some English; ask him for his recommendations on local bands. This is also a good place to pick up flyers for live music events. (📞06-6534-7411; www.flakerecords.com; No 201, 2nd fl, Sono Yotsubashi Bldg, 1-11-9 Minami-Horie, Nishi-ku; 🕙noon-9pm; Ⓢ Yotsubashi line to Yotsubashi, exit 6)

Village Vanguard

BOOKS

28 🔒 Map p114, B1

Village Vanguard bills itself as an 'exciting' bookstore, and it's a great starting point for fun, nontraditional, pop- and street-inspired mementos of your time in Japan. Between the cluttered book and magazine racks are offbeat T-shirts and accessories, novelty gifts, homewares and more. (ヴィレッジヴァンガード; www.village-v.co.jp; 1-10-28 Nishi-Shinsaibashi, Chūō-ku; 🕙11am-11pm; Ⓢ Midō-suji line to Shinsaibashi, exit 7)

Orange Street

FASHION & ACCESSORIES

29 🔒 Map p114, A2

In the trendy Minami-Horie district, this street is lined with fashionable streetwear boutiques. There's more on the side streets (along with plenty of cafes). (立花通り, Tachibana-dōri; Minami-Horie, Nishi-ku; Ⓢ Yotsubashi line to Yotsubashi, exit 6)

Osaka Takashimaya

DEPARTMENT STORE

30 🔒 Map p114, B4

The flagship of a long-running Osaka-based department store stocks

Shopping in Amerika-Mura (p115)

mostly international brands, though the homewares selection on the 6th floor is worth a look for local finds. The basement food hall is also good.

(大阪タカシマヤ; www.takashimaya. co.jp/osaka; 5-1-5 Namba, Chūō-ku; 10am-8pm; S Midō-suji line to Namba, exit 4)

Top Sights
Osaka-jō

Getting There

🚃 JR Loop line to Morinomiya or Osaka-jō; Keihin line to Temmabashi.

🚇 Tanimachi line to Temmabashi or Tanimachi 4-chōme; Chūō line to Tanimachi 4-chōme or Morinomiya.

After unifying Japan in the late 16th century, General Toyotomi Hideyoshi built this castle (1583) as a display of power, using, it's said, the labour of 100,000 workers. Although the present structure is a 1931 concrete reconstruction (refurbished 1997), it's nonetheless quite a sight, looming dramatically over the surrounding park and moat. Inside, a museum displays historical artefacts.

Don't Miss

The Castle Walls

Hideyoshi's original granite structure was said to be impregnable, yet it was destroyed in 1614 by the armies of Tokugawa Ieyasu (the founder of the Tokugawa shogunate). Ieyasu had the castle rebuilt – using the latest advancements to create terrifically imposing walls of enormous stones. The largest are estimated to weigh over 100 tonnes; others are engraved with the crests of feudal lords.

The Turrets & Gates

There are 13 structures on the castle grounds that date to the 17th-century reconstruction of the castle. **Sengan-yagura** (千貫櫓, Sengan Turret), next to **Ote-mon** (大手門) – the main gate, on the western side of the castle – and **Inui-yagura** (乾櫓, Inui Turret), on the northwest corner of the grounds, are the oldest: both date to 1620.

The Main Keep & Museum

By the 20th century most of the castle was in ruins. Osaka citizens raised money themselves to rebuild the main keep; in 1931 the new tower was revealed, with bright white walls and glittering gold-leaf tigers stalking the eaves. Inside, a museum displays historical artefacts, paintings, scrolls and suits of armour from the feudal era.

The Grounds

From the 8th-floor observatory inside the main keep there are excellent views of the sprawling, grassy grounds of the castle. For local residents, these grounds are the ultimate draw of the historical structure. Where soldiers once trained, families and couples now enjoy picnics and strolls.

COWARDLION/SHUTTERSTOCK ©

大阪城; Osaka Castle

www.osakacastle.net

1-1 Osaka-jō, Chūō-ku

grounds/castle keep free/¥600

⏱ 9am-5pm, to 7pm Aug

☑ Top Tips

▶ You can take an elevator up to the 5th floor of the keep, but you have to hike the rest of the way to the 8th floor (visitors with disabilities can take the elevator to the 8th floor).

▶ Return at night to see the castle lit with floodlights.

▶ Visit the grounds on a warm weekend and you might catch local musicians staging casual shows on the lawns.

✗ Take a Break

Vendors gather outside the main gate, selling street food such as *tako-yaki* and hotdogs.

Pick up more gourmet picnic supplies at bakery **Gout** (グウ; 1-1-10 Honmachi, Chūō-ku; ⏱ 7.30am-8pm Fri-Wed).

Top Sights
Tōdai-ji & Nara-kōen

Getting There

🚃 From Kyoto Station, take the Kintetsu or JR Nara line, 35 to 50 minutes.

🚃 From Osaka Namba Station, take the Kintetsu or JR Kansai line, 30 to 45 minutes.

The compact city of Nara (奈良) was Japan's first permanent capital and is well worth exploring on a day trip from either Kyoto or Osaka. Nara's star attraction is the Daibutsu (Great Buddha), one of the largest bronze Buddha images in the world and centrepiece of Tōdai-ji, a soaring temple that presides over the deer-filled green expanse of Nara-kōen.

Daibutsu (Great Buddha) statue

Don't Miss

Nara-kōen (Nara Park)

Tōdai-ji sits within Nara-kōen (奈良公園), a fine park that occupies much of the eastern side of the city and is home to many of Nara's most important temples, shrines and museums, as well as about 1200 deer. In pre-Buddhist times the deer were considered messengers of the gods and today enjoy the status of National Treasures, roaming the park seeking food from tourists.

Daibutsu-den (Great Buddha Hall)

A Unesco World Heritage Site, Tōdai-ji was built by order of Emperor Shōmu during the Nara period (710–784) and the complex was finally completed in 798, after the capital had been moved from Nara to Kyoto. The temple's Daibutsu-den (大仏殿) is among the largest wooden buildings on earth, with a length of 57m and a height of 48.74m.

Daibutsu (Great Buddha)

Within the Daibutsu-den sits the Great Buddha itself. The Daibutsu (大仏) is a huge statue originally cast in 746, though it has been recast several times over the centuries and has taken a beating from earthquakes and fires. It stands 14.98m high, and consists of 437 tonnes of bronze and 130kg of gold.

Pillar with Hole

Behind the Daibutsu is a pillar with a 50cm hole through its base (the size of one of the Daibutsu's nostrils). It's said that if you can squeeze through the hole, you are assured of enlightenment.

Nandai-mon Statues

The great south gate of Tōdai-ji contains two fierce-looking Niō guardians. These recently restored wooden images, carved in the 13th century by the famed sculptor Unkei, are some of the finest wooden statues in all of Japan.

東大寺

406-1 Zōshi-chō

Daibutsu-den admission ¥500, combination ticket with Tōdai-ji Museum ¥800

⊙Daibutsu-den 8am-4.30pm Nov-Feb, to 5pm Mar & Oct, 7.30am-5.30pm Apr-Sep

☑ Top Tips

▶ The deer sometimes harass and chase people with food; keep your snacks out of reach.

▶ Nara has two train stations. Kintetsu Nara Station is closer to the entrance of Nara-kōen (about 5 minutes' walk). JR Pass holders will want to use the JR line; JR Nara Station is about 20 minutes' walk from Nara-kōen.

✕ Take a Break

The thatched-roof teahouse **Mizuya-chaya** (水谷茶屋; ☏07542-22-0627; 30 Kasugano-chō; ⊙10am-4pm Thu-Tue) is good for a bowl of udon or cup of *matcha* (powdered green tea).

Explore

Kita

This district is the city's centre of gravity by day in office buildings, department stores and shopping complexes – plus the transit hubs of JR Osaka and Hankyū Umeda Stations (and the multiple train and subway lines converging here). While there are few great attractions here, there is plenty of big-city bustle both on street level and in the extensive network of underground passages below.

The Sights in a Day

☼ Start the day off shopping around Umeda; work your way around **Daimaru Umeda** (p138), stocking up on clothing and homewares before heading over to **Hep Five** (p137) for youth-oriented fashion and a spin on the Ferris wheel. Don't miss **Hankyū Umeda** (p136) for designer homewares and gourmet food. Give your feet a rest and pick a lunch spot at **Eki Marché** (p132).

☼ After lunch, head over to **O-hatsu Ten-jin** (p132) to pay your respects to star-crossed lovers Ohatsu and Tokubei before grabbing a coffee at **Moto** (p135), then visit the **Museum of Oriental Ceramics** (p131) to check out the excellent collection. Spend the rest of the afternoon taking in the views at the **Umeda Sky Building** (p131) and 20th-century art at the **National Museum of Art** (p132).

☾ Once you've had your fill of artworks, make your way to **Beer Belly** (p134) to sample the fantastic brews by Minoh. Head back to Osaka Station and finish up the day with *okonomiyaki* (savoury pancakes) at **Yukari** (p133).

 **Best of Osaka**

Eating

Eki Marché (p132)

Ganko Umeda Honten (p133)

Yukari (p133)

Drinking & Nightlife

Beer Belly (p134)

Moto Coffee (p135)

Frenz Frenzy (p135)

Getting There

🚃 **Train** In Kita you'll find the transit hubs of JR Osaka and Hankyū Umeda Stations (and multiple train and subway lines converge here).

A · B · C · D

1

Shin-Osaka
Station (2.8km)

21

Nakazakichō
S

Umeda Sky
Building
2

KITA-KU

27

6

CHAYAMACHI

19

23

Hankyū
Umeda

Jr Loop Line

**DŌYAMA-
CHŌ**

Underground Passage to
Umeda Sky Building

11

8 10

Miyakojima-dōri

15

2

17

22

24

Osaka Visitors
Information Center
Umeda

Umeda
S

Hankyū-Higashi Arcade

14

20

JR Kōbe Line

JR Osaka
S

Higashi
Umeda
S

25 5

Hanshin
Umeda

7

JR Kyoto Line

Umesan-kōji

UMEDA

Midō-suji

3

Jr Loop Line

Nishi-
Umeda
S

9

18

3

SONEZAKI

O-hatsu Ten-jin

Eki-mae
Dai-1 Bldg

16

Eki-mae
Dai-2 Bldg

Eki-mae
Dai-3 Bldg

Kita-
Shinchi

SHINCHI

For reviews see

⊙ Sights	p131
✕ Eating	p132
🍷 Drinking	p134
☆ Entertainment	p136
🔒 Shopping	p136

26

**KITA-
SHINCHI**

4

Dōjima-gawa

Keihan
Watanabebashi

Keihan
Oebashi

Keihan
Naniwabashi

Museum
of Oriental
Ceramics

1

Tosabori-gawa

Midō-suji

Naka-
no-
shima

National
Museum
of Art, Osaka

4

Higobashi
S

Keihan Yodoyabashi
S

Keihan Main Line

Kitahama
S

13

5

**NAKO-NO-
SHIMA**

12

Yotsubashi-suji

Yodoyabashi
S

N

0 —————— 200 m
0 —————— 0.1 miles

Umeda Sky Building

Sights

Museum of Oriental Ceramics   MUSEUM

1 Map p130, D4

This museum has one of the world's finest collections of Chinese and Korean ceramics, with smaller galleries of Japanese ceramics and Chinese snuff bottles. At any one time, approximately 400 of the gorgeous pieces from the permanent collection are on display, and there are often special exhibits (with an extra charge). The permanent collection has good English descriptions. (大阪市立東洋陶磁美術館; www.moco.or.jp; 1-1-26 Naka-no-shima; adult/student/child ¥500/300/free;

⏱9.30am-5pm, closed Mon; Ⓢ Midō-suji line to Yodoyabashi, exit 1)

Umeda Sky Building   NOTABLE BUILDING

2 Map p130, A1

Osaka's landmark Sky Building (1993) resembles a 40-storey, space-age Arc de Triomphe. Twin towers are connected at the top by a 'floating garden' (really a garden-free observation deck), which was constructed on the ground and then hoisted up. The 360-degree city views from here are breathtaking day or night. Getting there is half the fun – an escalator in a see-through tube takes you up the last five storeys (not for vertigo sufferers). The architect, Hara Hiroshi, also designed Kyoto Station (p28). (梅田スカイビル; www.kuchu-teien.com; 1-1-88 Ōyodonaka, Kita-ku; admission ¥700; ⊙observation decks 10am-10.30pm, last entry 10pm; 🚆JR Osaka, north central exit)

O-hatsu Ten-jin

SHINTO SHRINE

 3 Map p130, C3

Hiding in plain sight amid the skyscrapers of Umeda, this 1300-year-old shrine owes its fame to one of Japan's best-known tragic plays (based on true events). Star-crossed lovers O-hatsu, a prostitute, and Tokubei, a merchant's apprentice, rather than live apart, committed double suicide here in 1703, to remain together forever in the afterlife. The current shrine was constructed in 1957 (after WWII destroyed the previous one); it's popular with couples, who come to pray for strength in love – and happier endings. (お初天神, Tsuyu-no-Ten-jinsha; 📞06-6311-0895; www.tuyutenjin.com; 2-5-4 Sonezaki, Kita-ku; admission free; ⊙6am-midnight; Ⓢ Tanimachi line to Higashi-Umeda, exit 7, exit 15, 🚆JR Osaka, Sakurabashi exit)

National Museum of Art, Osaka

MUSEUM

 4 Map p130, A5

Originally built for Expo '70, this underground construction by architect Cesar Pelli now houses Japan's fourth national museum. There's a decent collection of 20th-century works by Japanese artists. The building – like a submarine, with walls over 3m thick and light filtering down through skylights above the lobby – is interesting too. The entrance is marked by a large sculpture of steel tubes, said to resemble a butterfly. The museum is located towards the western end of Naka-no-shima. (国立国際美術館; www.nmao.go.jp; 4-2-55 Naka-no-shima, Kita-ku; adult/student/child ¥430/170/free, special exhibitions extra; ⊙10am-5pm, to 8pm Fri & Sat, closed Mon; Ⓢ Yotsubashi line to Higobashi, exit 3)

Eating

Eki Marché

FOOD HALL ¥

 5 Map p130, B2

This excellent collection of wallet-friendly eateries and takeaway counters is on the southwestern side of JR Osaka Station. Top picks include Kaiten Sushi Ganko, for conveyor-belt sushi, and **Kani Chahan-no-Mise** (かにチャーハンの店; 📞06-6341-3103; Eki Maré, Osaka Station City, Kita-ku; mains from ¥680; ⊙10am-10.30pm; 😊; 🚆JR Osaka, Sakurabashi exit), for delectable crab fried rice. (エキマルシェ大阪; www.ekimaru.com; Osaka Station City, Kita-ku; ⊙10am-10pm; 🚆JR Osaka, Sakurabashi exit)

Kaiten Sushi Ganko

SUSHI ¥¥

This reliable *kaiten-sushi* (conveyor-belt sushi) shop is a popular choice for many a hungry commuter, meaning the two whirring tracks of plates are continuously restocked with appealing options. It can get crowded at meal times. It's inside JR Osaka's Eki Marché food court (see 5 Map p130, B2). (回転寿司がんこ; ☏06-4799-6811; Eki Maré, Osaka Station City, Kita-ku; plates ¥130-735; ☺11am-11pm; 🗐; 🚇JR Osaka, Sakurabashi exit)

Ganko Umeda Honten
JAPANESE ¥¥

6 Map p130, B1

At the main branch of this Osaka institution, a large dining hall serves a wide variety of set-course meals and sushi (à la carte or in sets), reasonably priced and using traditional, quality ingredients. It's on the street along the western side of Hankyū Umeda Station. Look for the logo of the guy wearing a headband. (がんこ梅田本店; ☏06-6376-2001; www.gankofood.co.jp; 1-5-11 Shibata, Kita-ku; meals ¥780-5000; ☺11.30am-4am Mon-Sat, to midnight Sun; 🗐; 🚇Hankyū Umeda)

Yukari
OKONOMIYAKI ¥¥

7 Map p130, C3

This popular restaurant in the Ohatsutenjin-dōri arcade serves up that great Osaka favourite, *okonomiyaki* (savoury pancakes), cooked on a griddle before you. There are lots to choose from on the picture menu, including veg options, but the *tokusen mikkusu yaki* (mixed *okonomiyaki* with fried pork, shrimp and squid; ¥1080) is a classic. Look for red and white signage out front. (ゆかり; ☏06-6311-0214; www.yukarichan.co.jp; 2-14-13 Sōnezaki, Kita-ku; okonomiyaki ¥800-1460;

☺11am-1am; 🖉🗐; 🚇Tanimachi line to Higashi-Umeda, exit 4, 🚇JR Osaka, south central exit)

Robatayaki Isaribi
IZAKAYA ¥¥

Head downstairs to this spirited, friendly *izakaya* (pub eatery) for standards such as skewered meats, seafood, veggies fresh off the grill and giant pieces of *tori no karaage* (fried chicken). The best seats are at semi-circular counters, where your chef will serve you using a *looooong* paddle. It's next to Ganko Umeda Honten (see 6 Map p130, B1). (炉ばた焼き漁火; ☏06-6373-2969; www.rikimaru-group.com/shop/isaribi.html; 1-5-12 Shibata, Kita-ku; dishes ¥325; ☺5-11.15pm; 🗐; 🚇Midō-suji line to Umeda, exit 2, 🚇Hankyū Umeda)

Hankyū Sanbangai
FOOD HALL ¥

8 Map p130, C2

Beneath Hankyū Umeda Station is a long string of Japanese and international restaurants, as well as shops selling cakes, pastries and chocolates. (阪急三番街; www.h-sanbangai.com; 2nd basement fl, Hankyū Umeda Station, Kita-ku; ☺10am-11pm; 🚇Hankyū Umeda)

Shinkiraku
TEMPURA ¥¥

9 Map p130, B3

This tempura specialist in the Hilton Plaza packs 'em in at lunchtime. The *ebishio-tendon* (shrimp tempura over rice; ¥980) set is plenty filling. Take the escalator down to the 2nd basement floor, go right and look for the small English sign. (新善楽;

☎06-6345-3461; 2nd basement fl, Hilton Plaza East, 1-8-16 Umeda, Kita-ku; set meals ¥980-4500; ⏰11am-2.30pm & 5-11pm Mon-Fri, 11am-2.30pm & 4-10pm Sat, Sun & holidays; ☺◉; §Yotsubashi line to Nishi-Umeda, exit 6, ℝJR Osaka, south central exit)

Satoyama Dining
JAPANESE ¥¥

10 ✕ Map p130, C2

Satoyama's all-you-can-eat 'Viking' (buffet) setup lets you choose from mostly Japanese home-style dishes, while enjoying great city views from the picture windows. After 8.30pm the dinner price drops to ¥2160; there are discounts for kids. You can enter the Hankyū Terminal Building directly from Hankyū Umeda Station. (里山

> ### ◯ Local Life
> **Umeda Hagakure**
>
> Two storeys underground and three decades old, this **shop** (梅田はがくれ; Map p130, C3; ☎06-6341-1409; 2nd basement fl, Osaka Eki-mae Dai-3 Bldg, 1-1 Umeda, Kita-ku; noodles ¥600-1100; ⏰11am-2.45pm & 5-7.45pm Mon-Fri, 11am-2.30pm Sat & Sun; §Tanimachi line to Higashi-Umeda, exit 8, ℝJR Osaka, south central exit) is cramped and work-manlike, but locals queue for udon noodles made before your eyes. Cold noodles are the speciality; try refreshing *nama-jōyu* (with soy sauce, ground daikon (radish) and *sudachi* lime; ¥600) or *tenzaru* (with tempura; ¥1100). Order from the picture menu, and get hand-gestured eating instructions from the owner.

ダイニング; ☎050-5798-6499; 17th fl, Hankyū Terminal Bldg, 1-1-4 Shibata, Kita-ku; lunch/dinner for up to 1½ hours ¥1950/2920; ⏰11am-11.30pm; ☺✐♿; ℝHankyū Umeda)

Umekita Dining
FOOD HALL ¥¥

11 ✕ Map p130, B2

There are dozens of restaurants (including Japanese, French, Spanish and Chinese), cafes, bakeries and sweets shops on the upper floors of the Grand Front Osaka shopping mall. Most are options are midrange, with menus out front, making this a convenient place to shop around for a meal. The basement food hall **Umekita Cellar** has cheaper vendors and takeaway counters. (グランフロント大阪; www.gfo-sc.jp; 7th-9th fl, Grand Front Osaka South Bldg, Kita-ku; prices vary; ⏰11am-11pm; ℝJR Osaka, north central exit, ℝHankyū Umeda)

Drinking

Beer Belly
CRAFT BEER

12 🍺 Map p130, B5

Beer Belly is run by Osaka's best microbrewery, Minoh Beer. There are 10 taps and one hand pump featuring Minoh's award-winning classics and seasonal offerings (pints from ¥1000). Pick up a copy here of Osaka's *Craft Beer Map* to further your local beer adventures. From the subway exit, double back and take the road that curves behind the APA Hotel. (www.beerbelly.jp/tosabori; 1-1-31 Tosabori, Nishi-ku;

Sushi

⏱5pm-2am Mon-Fri, 3-11pm Sat, 3-9pm Sun; Ⓢ Yotsubashi line to Higobashi, exit 3)

Moto Coffee
CAFE

13 Map p130, D5

Sitting pretty in a small, whitewashed building next to the Kyū-Yodogawa, Moto serves quality coffee drinks (from ¥450) on its riverside terrace (or upstairs if the terrace is full). (モトコーヒー; 📞06-4706-3788; 2-1-1 Kitahama, Chūō-ku; ⏱noon-7pm; Ⓢ Sakai-suji line to Kitahama, exit 26)

Frenz Frenzy
GAY & LESBIAN

14 Map p130, D2

Frenz Frenzy calls itself a 'rainbow haven' and it means that literally:

the whole place is awash in colour (including the front door, thankfully, because otherwise it would be impossible to find). Run by long-time expat Sari-chan, this is a welcoming first port of call for gay and lesbian travellers. There's no cover and drinks start at ¥500. (📞06-6311-1386; http://frenz-frenzy.website; 18-14 Kamiyama-chō, Kita-ku; ⏱8pm-1am; Ⓢ Tanimachi line to Higashi-Umeda, exit 3)

G Physique
GAY

15 Map p130, D2

This small, long-running gay bar in Dōyama-chō is welcoming to locals and visitors alike. There's no cover charge and drinks are reasonably priced. (1st fl, Sanyo-Kaikan Bldg, 8-23 Dōyama-chō, Kita-ku; ⏰from 7pm, closing time varies; ⓢTanimachi line to Higashi-Umeda, exit 3)

Kissa Madura

CAFE

16 Map p130, B3

Running for 70 years, Madura is a glorious time capsule of retro future styling, with tulip chairs, mirrors and chrome, and also vintage pricing – coffee costs just ¥250. (喫茶マヅラ; Basement fl, Eki-mae Dai-1 Bldg, 1-3-1 Umeda, Kita-ku; ⏰8am-11pm; ⓢYotsubashi line to Nishi-Umeda, exit 7a, ⓇJR Osaka, south central exit)

Craft Beer Base

BAR

17 Map p130, A2

In the shadow of the Umeda Sky Building, this bar and bottle shop specialises in local and international craft beers. Order and enjoy around the counter, or climb the narrow stairs to a simple white-walled room. There's a corkage fee of ¥350 to ¥500 for bottles if you drink in-house. (クラフト・ビア・ベース; www.craftbeerbase. com; 1-2-11 Ōyodo-minami, Kita-ku; draft beer ¥1000-1200; ⏰11am-11pm Fri-Wed, 5-11pm Thu; ⓢMidō-suji line to Umeda, exit 3, ⓇJR Osaka, north central exit)

Windows on the World

BAR

18 Map p130, B3

On the 35th floor of the Hilton, this upscale bar has excellent views and a good wine and whiskey list. Drinks run about ¥2000; there's also a ¥1750 per person table charge (¥1200 for hotel guests) and a 12% service charge. (ウィンドーズオンザワールド; 35th fl, Hilton Osaka, 1-8-8 Umeda, Kita-ku; ⏰5.30pm-12.30am Mon-Thu & Sun, to 1am Fri & Sat; ⓢYotsubashi line to Nishi-Umeda, exit 6, ⓇJR Osaka, south central exit)

Entertainment

Osaka Nōgaku Hall

THEATRE

19 Map p130, D1

A five-minute walk east of Hankyū Umeda Station, this theatre stages *nō* (stylised dance-drama) performances a few times each month. Look for the relief of a *nō* actor holding a fan on the facade. You'll need a Japanese speaker to call ahead about tickets. (大阪能楽会館; Osaka Nōgaku Kaikan; ☎06-6373-1726; http://nougaku.wixsite. com/nougaku; 2-3-17 Nakasaki-nishi, Kita-ku; tickets free-¥13,000; ⓢTanimachi line to Nakazakichō, exit 4, ⓇHankyū Umeda)

Shopping

Hankyū Umeda Department Store

DEPARTMENT STORE

20 Map p130, C2

Hankyū, which first opened in 1929, pioneered the now ubiquitous concept of the train station department store. One of Japan's largest department stores, 'Ume-Han' is also among the most fashion-forward, with a good selection of edgy Japanese designers on the 3rd floor. Head to the 7th floor for artisan homewares and the basement for a cornucopia of gourmet food items. (阪急梅田本店; www.hankyu-dept. co.jp/honten; 8-7 Kakuda-chō, Kita-ku; ⏰10am-8pm Sun-Thu, to 9pm Fri & Sat; Ⓢ Midō-suji line to Umeda, exit 6, 🚇 Hankyū Umeda)

Maruzen & Junkudō Umeda
BOOKS

21 🔒 Map p130, C1

This is the largest bookstore in Osaka, the result of two established chains joining forces. There's a big range of English-language books (on the 6th floor) and travel guides (3rd floor). It's in the Andō Tadao–designed Chaska Chayamachi building. (丸善&ジュンク堂書店梅田店; www.junkudo.co.jp; Chaska Chayamachi Bldg, 7-20 Chayamachi, Kita-ku; ⏰10am-10pm; 🚇 Hankyū Umeda)

Lucua
DEPARTMENT STORE

22 🔒 Map p130, B2

A big selection of stylish Japanese and international brands, on the northern side of JR Osaka Station. (ルクア; www. lucua.jp; North Gate Bldg, 3-1-3 Umeda, Kita-ku; ⏰shops 10am-9pm, dining 11am-11pm; 🚇 JR Osaka, Midō-suji north exit)

Kōjitsu-sansō
SPORTS & OUTDOORS

23 🔒 Map p130, B1

If you need a new backpack or any other kind of outdoor gear, head to this excellent shop in the Grand Front complex. (好日山荘; www.kojitusanso.jp; 5th fl,

Grand Front North Bldg, 3-1 Ōfuka-chō, Kita-ku; ⏰10am-9pm; 🚇 JR Osaka, north central exit)

Hep Five
DEPARTMENT STORE

24 🔒 Map p130, C2

Trendy, youthful labels on the first six floors; fast-food restaurants, cafes and arcades on the upper floors; and a bright red Ferris wheel on the roof. (www.hepfive.jp; 5-15 Kakuda-chō, Kita-ku; ⏰shops 11am-9pm, dining & entertainment to 11pm; Ⓢ Midō-suji line to Umeda, exit 6, 🚇 Hankyū Umeda)

◯ Local Life
Nakazaki-chō

Nakazaki-chō (中崎町), 1km northeast of Umeda Station, is one of the rare neighbourhoods in Osaka that still has many wooden buildings predating WWII (the neighbourhood was spared by bombs). Many, however, were in a state of decline, until local performing artist Amanto Jun set about restoring one such structure, turning it into the cafe and creative hive **Salon de Amanto Tenjin** (サロン・ド・アマント天人; http://amanto.jp; 1-7-26 Nakazaki-nishi, Kita-ku; ⏰noon-10pm; 📶, Ⓢ Tanimachi line to Nakazakichō, exit 4). Others followed, and now the district is full of cute cafes and *zakka* (miscellaneous goods) stores. It's a very different vibe from the shops and cafes of Minami, and worth a look. Take the Tanimachi subway line to Nakazakichō and take exit 4.

Top Tip

Shopping at Osaka Station

Osaka Station is ringed by malls and department stores – they're all interconnected by underground passages, making the Umeda district one big shopping conurbation. You'll find outlets of all of Japan's most popular national chains here, like Uniqlo, Muji, Tokyu Hands and **Yodobashi electronics** (ヨドバシ梅田; Map p130, B2; www.yodobashi-umeda.com; 1-1 Ōfuka-chō, Kita-ku; ⊙shops 9.30am-10pm, restaurants 11am-11pm; Ⓢ Midō-suji line to Umeda, exit 4, Ⓡ JR Osaka, Midō-suji north exit), along with literally hundreds of fashion boutiques.

Daimaru Umeda   DEPARTMENT STORE

25 🔒   Map p130, B2

This huge Umeda branch of the classic Kansai department store anchors Osaka Station's southern side. On the upper floors you'll find branches of Tokyu Hands, Uniqlo, and the Pokemon character goods shop, **Pokemon Centre** (ポケットモンスター; 13th fl, Daimaru Department Store, 3-1-1 Umeda, Kita-ku; ⊙10am-8pm; Ⓡ JR Osaka, south central

exit). (大丸梅田店; 🕽 06-6343-1231; www. daimaru.co.jp/umedamise; South Gate Bldg, 3-1-1 Umeda, Kita-ku; ⊙10am-8pm; Ⓡ JR Osaka, south central exit)

Junkudō   BOOKS

26 🔒   Map p130, B4

This large bookshop has a great selection of English-language books (on the 3rd floor) and English travel guides (2nd floor). It's inside the Dōjima Avanza Building, about 10 minutes' walk from JR Osaka Station. (ジュンク堂書店; www.junkudo.co.jp; Dōjima Avanza Bldg, 1-6-20 Dōjima, Kita-ku; ⊙10am-9pm; Ⓡ JR Tōzai line to Kita-Shinchi, exit 2)

NU Chayamachi   DEPARTMENT STORE

27 🔒   Map p130, C1

This series of stylish shopping centres is linked by brick paths lined with trees; it's a popular place to hang-out on weekends. In addition to men's and women's fashions, look for musical instruments and a large Tower Records store. (NU茶屋町; http://nu-chayamachi.com; 10-12 Chayamachi, Kita-ku; ⊙fashion shops 11am-9pm, Tower Records to 11pm, restaurants to midnight; Ⓡ Hankyū Umeda)

阪急 ⑭

Hankyū Umeda Department Store (p136)

The Best of
Kyoto & Osaka

Kimino and obi (sash)
JIRAT TEPARAKSA/SHUTTERSTOCK ©

Best Walks
A Philosophical Meander

The Walk

Northern Higashiyama is home to some of the city's best sightseeing with magical Buddhist temple complexes spread out like a string of pearls along the Path of Philosophy, known as Tetsugaku-no-michi in Japanese. The path follows a cherry-blossom-lined canal and offers some of the prettiest scenery in Kyoto – a big achievement for a city known for its postcard-perfect streetscapes. Dip in and out of temples as you stroll along the Path of Philosophy, taking time to ponder as did the namesake 20th-century philosopher Nishida Kitarō, before finishing your walk with the stunning sight of Ginkaku-ji.

Start Keage Station

Finish Ginkaku-ji-Michi bus stop

Length About 6km; four hours

Take a Break

Hinode Udon (p88)

TODYKRUB/SHUTTERSTOCK ©

Path of Philosophy (p82), Kyoto

1 Konchi-in

Start at Keage Station on the Tōzai subway line, walk downhill, cross the pedestrian overpass, head back uphill and go through the tunnel under the old funicular tracks. This leads to a narrow street that winds towards **Konchi-in** (p85), a lovely subtemple of Nanzen-ji with an excellent garden.

2 Nanzen-ji

Just past Konchi-in, take a right on the main road and walk up through the gate into **Nanzen-ji** (p76). Take your time to roam around its expansive grounds and don't miss the classic Zen garden, Leaping Tiger Garden. Check out the main hall and sip a cup of *matcha* while admiring the waterfall.

3 Nanzen-ji Oku-no-in

Continue east, up the slope and you'll soon see the brick Sōsui aqueduct on your right; cross under this, take a quick left and walk up the hill towards the mountains. You'll come first to the lovely Kōtoku-an subtemple. Beyond this, the trail enters the woods. Follow it up to the secluded **Nanzen-ji Oku-no-in** (p83), a tiny shrine built around a waterfall.

④ Eikan-dō

Return the way you came and exit the north side of Nanzen-ji, following the road through a gate. You'll soon come to **Eikan-dō** (p82), a large temple famous for its artworks and interesting architecture. Climb up to the top of the pagoda for stunning views over the city.

⑤ Path of Philosophy (Tetsugaku-no-michi)

At the corner just beyond Eikan-dō, a sign in English and Japanese points up the hill to the **Path of Philosophy** (Tetsugaku-no-michi; p82), which is the pedestrian path that heads north along the canal. This is one of the most picturesque spots in the city, particularly in cherry-blossom season.

⑥ Ginkaku-ji

Continue wandering along the beautiful Path of Philosophy and then follow the narrow side streets north to **Ginkaku-ji** (p78), the famed Silver Pavilion. Don't miss the superb raked garden and walking path that leads through tall pine trees up the mountainside.

Best Walks
Southern Higashiyama Highlights

🏃 The Walk

The concentration of sights in Southern Higashiyama can be a little daunting, with so many temples, shrines, museums and craft shops crammed into one neighbourhood. This walk starts in the southern part of the neighbourhood at Kiyomizu-dera temple and works its way directly north to finish off at the peaceful Shōren-in temple with its beautiful garden. In between, the walk takes you through traditional neighborhoods lined with *machiya* (traditional Japanese houses) home to boutiques and teahouses, detours through atmospheric backstreets and into temples – some well-known, others a bit more hidden – cuts through Maruyama Park and winds up with a cup of *matcha* overlooking a temple garden.

Start Gojō-zaka bus stop

Finish Higashiyama Station

Length 5km; four hours

🍴 Take Break
Hisago (p70)

Kiyomizu-dera (p58), Kyoto

JANNOON028/SHUTTERSTOCK ©

① Kiyomizu-dera

From the starting point at Gojō-zaka bus stop on Higashiōji-dōri, walk up Gojō-zaka slope. Head uphill until you reach the first fork in the road; bear right and continue up Chawan-zaka (Teapot Lane). At the top of the hill, you'll come to **Kiyomizu-dera** (p58), a stunning temple perched high on a hill overlooking Kyoto.

② Kasagi-ya

After touring Kiyomizu-dera, exit along Kiyomizu-michi. Continue down the hill and take a right at the four-way intersection down stone-paved steps. This is Sannen-zaka, where you will find tiny **Kasagi-ya** (p70), which has been serving tea and sweets for as long as anyone can remember. It's on the left, just below a vending machine.

③ Ninen-zaka & Sannen-zaka

Take it slow exploring the hidden lanes and streets in this area. Half-way down **Sannen-zaka** (p69), the road curves to the left. Follow it a short distance, then go right down a flight of steps into **Ninen-zaka** (p69). At the end of Ninen-zaka zigzag left (at the vending machines) then right (just past the car park) and continue north.

④ Kōdai-ji

Very soon, on your left, you'll come to the entrance to Ishibei-kōji – perhaps the most beautiful street in Kyoto. Detour to explore this, then retrace your steps and continue north, passing almost immediately the entrance to **Kōdai-ji** (p67) on the right up a long flight of stairs. Wander the exceptional gardens here designed by famed landscape architect Kobori Enshū.

⑤ Maruyama-kōen

After Kōdai-ji continue north to the T-junction; turn right here and then take a quick left. You'll cross the pedestrian arcade that leads to Ōtani cemetery and then descend into **Maruyama-kōen** (p66). Look out for the giant Gion shidare-zakura, Kyoto's most famous cherry tree, and take some time to people-watch.

⑥ Chion-in

From the park, you can head west into the grounds of Yasaka-jinja. Then return to the park and head north to tour the grounds of **Chion-in** (p60). Note the two-storey San-mon temple gate, the largest in Japan, and visit the giant bell, which weighs 70 tonnes and was cast in 1633.

⑦ Shōren-in

From here it's a quick walk to **Shōren-in** (p66). This is one of the finest temples and gardens in the city, and is a little more off the main tourist trail compared to the others. Sip *matcha* and admire the garden. From Shōren-in walk down to Sanjō-dōri to Higashiyama Station.

Best
History

Kyoto forms a vast living textbook of Japanese history: almost everywhere you step, an event took place that shaped the nation we know as Japan. Exploring the sights of Kyoto today is like stepping back through Japan's history. Osaka's history may not be as rich but is no less important and the city has always played a vital role in Japan as a key port and mercantile centre.

COWARDLION/SHUTTERSTOCK ©

Kyoto's History

From the 8th century until the late 19th century, Kyoto's history was almost synonymous with Japanese history. Kyoto was literally the stage where the great events of Japanese history unfolded. This is where emperors and shoguns vied for power. This is where the main religious sects were born and popularised. And this is where the traditional arts of Japan were polished to their present-day perfection.

As Kyoto heads into the future, the real challenge is to preserve its ancient history while meeting the desires of its citizens for economic development and modern convenience.

Osaka's History

Osaka (originally called 'Naniwa', a name still heard today) has been a key port and mercantile centre from the beginning of Japan's recorded history. From the 6th century onwards, it became Japan's base for trade with Korea and China – a gateway for goods but also ideas, such as Buddhism and

Worth a Trip

One of the highlights of northeast Kyoto, **Shūgaku-in Rikyū Imperial Villa** (修学院離宮; www.kunaicho.go.jp; Shūgaku-in, Yabusoe, Sakyō-ku; 🚌 Kyoto City bus 5 from Kyoto Station to Shūgakuinrikyū-michi) was designed as a lavish summer retreat for the imperial family. Its gardens, with their views over the city, are worth the trouble it takes to visit. Eighty-minute tours (in Japanese) start at 9am, 10am, 11am, 1.30pm and 3pm from Tuesday to Sunday; try to arrive early. English audio guides are free of charge. You must be over 18 years to enter and you will need to bring your passport for ID.

JULIANG2000/SHUTTERSTOCK ©

Shūgaku-in Rikyū Imperial Villa, Kyoto

empire-building, and new technologies.

In the late 16th century, Osaka rose to prominence when the warlord Toyotomi Hideyoshi, having unified all of Japan after centuries of civil war, chose Osaka as the site for his castle. During the Edo period (1603–1868) Osaka served as Japan's largest distribution centre for rice (which was akin to currency at the time), earning it the nickname 'Japan's Kitchen.'

Today commerce remains vital to Osaka – it is the business hub of western Japan.

Historical Sights, Kyoto

Nijō-jō A symbol of the military might of the Tokugawa shoguns. (p38)

Kyoto Imperial Palace The former residence of the emperor of Japan. (p96)

Sentō Gosho Palace A grand residence for retired emperors. (p101)

Gion The city's former pleasure district and geisha quarter. (p62)

Historical Sights, Osaka

O-hatsu Ten-jin 1300-year-old Shinto shrine dedicated to star-crossed lovers. (p132)

Osaka-jō Castle built by General Toyotomi Hideyoshi as a display of power after unifying Japan in the late 16th century. (p125)

Best
Food

Kyoto is one of the world's great food cities. In fact, when you consider atmosphere, service and quality, it's hard to think of a city where you get more bang for your dining buck. You can pretty much find a great dining option in any neighbourhood but the majority of the best spots are clustered downtown.

Kyoto Specialities

Kaiseki (Japanese haute cuisine) This is the pinnacle of refined dining, where ingredients, preparation, setting and presentation come together to create a dining experience quite unlike any other. It is a largely vegetarian affair (though fish is often served) and is usually eaten in the private room of a *ryōtei* (traditional, high-class Japanese restaurant) or ryokan.

Tofu-ryōri Kyoto is also famed for its tofu (soybean curd), a result of the city's excellent water and large population of (theoretically) vegetarian Buddhist monks. There are numerous tofu-ya-san (tofu makers) scattered throughout the city and a legion of exquisite *yudōfu* (tofu cooked in a pot) restaurants – many are concentrated in Northern Higashiyama along the roads around Nanzen-ji and in the Arashiyama area.

Osaka Specialities

Tako-yaki These doughy dumplings stuffed with octopus (*tako* in Japanese) and grilled in specially made moulds are often sold as street food, served with pickled ginger, topped with savoury sauce, powdered *aonori* (seaweed), mayonnaise and bonito flakes and eaten with toothpicks. Nibble carefully first as the centre can be molten hot.

LONELY PLANET/LOTTIE DAVIES ©

☑ **Top Tips**

▶ Check out department store basement floors for gourmet shops, while the upper floors usually have a *resutoran-gai* (restaurant city).

▶ Many of Kyoto's elite *kaiseki* restaurants serve a delicious lunch set or bentō that cost a fraction of their normal dinner offerings.

Okonomiyaki Thick, savoury pancakes filled with shredded cabbage and your choice of meat, seafood, vegetables and more (the name means 'cook as you like'). Often prepared on a *teppan* (hot plate) set into your table, the cooked pancake is brushed with a savoury Worcestershire-style sauce, decoratively striped with mayonnaise and topped with dried bonito flakes, which seem to dance in the rising steam.

Kaiseki

Kikunoi, Kyoto Wonderful *kaiseki* in a classic setting. (p69)

Kitcho Arashiyama, Kyoto No-holds-barred *kaiseki* served in superb private rooms. (p107)

Roan Kikunoi, Kyoto Experimental and creative *kaiseki* in a downtown location. (p48)

Shoubentango-tei, Osaka Osaka-style *kaiseki* in a 100-year-old restaurant. (p117)

Noodles (Soba & Udon)

Honke Owariya, Kyoto Filling soba and udon in a quiet downtown spot. (p47)

Omen Kodai-ji, Kyoto Wonderful noodles in a smart setting in Southern Higashiyama. (p70)

Imai Honten, Osaka One of the oldest udon noodle specialists in Dōtombori. (p117)

Umeda Hagakure, Osaka Local favourite for cold noodles. (p134)

Ramen

Ippūdō, Kyoto Tasty Kyushu-style ramen and crispy *gyōza*. (p49)

Karako, Kyoto Delicious thick meaty soup and tender pork slices. (p86)

Kyoto Rāmen Kōji, Kyoto Choice of nine ramen joints in Kyoto Station. (p30)

Kinryū Ramen, Osaka People-watch in Dōtombori as you slurp back cheap noodles. (p118)

Sushi

Musashi Sushi, Kyoto Convenient and cheap downtown sushi-belt restaurant. (p49)

Kaiten Sushi Ganko, Osaka Convenient sushi spot for commuters. (p132)

Tempura

Shunsai Tempura Arima, Kyoto Friendly and approachable tempura in a family-run restaurant. (p46)

Yoshikawa, Kyoto Great tempura and a beautiful garden. (p48)

Shinkiraku, Osaka Popular tempura specialist in the Hilton Plaza. (p133)

Okonomiyaki

Yukari, Osaka Loads of *okonomiyaki* options at this favourite spot. (p133)

Chibō, Osaka City's most famous *okonomiyaki* spot with long queues. (p116)

Nishiki Warai, Kyoto Convenient casual eatery near Nishiki Market. (p50)

Kiraku, Kyoto A great option near Nanzen-ji. (p88)

Best
Shopping & Markets

Kyoto and Osaka have a fantastic variety of both traditional and modern shops, and some great markets. Whether you're looking for fans, kimonos and tea, or the latest electronics, hip fashion and ingenuous gadgets, these two cities have plenty to offer.

APPLES EYES STUDIO/SHUTTERSTOCK ©

Kyoto

Shopping neighbourhoods in Kyoto tend to be organised by specialities, which makes things easier if you're after specific items. Following are some of Kyoto's most important shopping streets and what you'll find there:

Teramachi-dōri, north of Oike-dōri Traditional Japanese crafts, tea-ceremony goods, green tea and antiques.

Teramachi-dōri, south of Shijō-dōri Electronics and computers.

Shijō-dōri, between Kawaramachi-dōri and Karasuma-dōri Department stores, fashion boutiques and traditional arts and crafts.

Osaka

Osaka is the biggest shopping destination in western Japan, with an overwhelming number of malls, department stores, shopping arcades, electronics dealers, boutiques and secondhand shops. Flea markets take place every month at shrines and temples, including O-hatsu Ten-jin and Shitennō-ji.

Denden Town (でんでんタウン) is Osaka's electronics district. While megastores like Bic Camera and Yodobashi have stolen its thunder, it has a retro-cool charm: a Super Mario Bros–style green pipe runs along the top of the street awning and stores sell old-school motherboards and other

 Top Tip

▶ Show your passport at 'Japan Tax-Free Shops'; visitors in Kyoto less than six months are exempt from the 8% consumption tax for purchases equal to or over ¥5000 for general items, and between ¥5000 and ¥500,000 for consumables. For more info, see http://tax-freeshop.jnto.go.jp/eng.

vintage parts. Most stores are closed on Wednesday.

Department Stores, Kyoto

Daimaru A sumptuous selection at this vast downtown store. (p40)

CARL FORBES/SHUTTERSTOCK ©

Nishiki Market (p36), Kyoto

Takashimaya An elegant and rich assortment of shops, along with great restaurants and a food floor to boggle the mind. (p54)

BAL For high-end fashion, and books on the basement floors. (p55)

Department Stores, Osaka

Hankyū Umeda Department Store Food, fashion and homewares in one of Japan's largest department stores. (p136)

Tokyu Hands Gadgets, crafts and homewares at this popular Osaka outpost. (p122)

Traditional Japanese Items, Kyoto

Wagami no Mise A beautiful selection of *washi* (Japanese handmade paper) at this downtown shop. (p54)

Zōhiko A wonderland for the lover of lacquerware. (p52)

Kyoto Handicraft Center The quality of goods at this one-stop handicraft shop is excellent. (p89)

Nishiki Market Kyoto Head here for traditional food-related gifts, including cooking implements, tea, sweets and sake. (p36)

Traditional Japanese Items, Osaka

Takashimaya The food floor is superb and the selection of kitchenware and dining ware on the 6th floor is not to be missed. (p54)

Dōguya-suji Arcade Market stalls crammed with cookware and kitchen goods. (p121)

Best
Culture

The cultural life of Kyoto was centred on the imperial court for over 1100 years. The court drew to it the finest artisans and craftspeople from across Japan, resulting in an incredibly rich cultural and artistic atmosphere. Today Kyoto is still home to many of Japan's best artists in every field, from textiles and bamboo craft to the tea ceremony.

ALEKSANDAR TODOROVIC/SHUTTERSTOCK ©

Kyoto's Arts & Crafts

Rightly described as Japan's cultural heart and soul, Kyoto is famous for keeping alive the flame of Japanese tradition. Almost all of Japan's traditional arts and crafts reached their peak of sophistication and elegance here. From kabuki to textiles, Kyoto's traditional arts and crafts reflect centuries of polishing and refinement in a city that was home to Japan's most discerning citizens for well over 1000 years.

Textiles

Kyoto is famous for its *kyō-yūzen* textiles. *Yūzen* is a method of silk-dyeing *(senshoku)* developed to perfection in the 17th century by fan painter Miyazaki Yūzen. *Kyō-yūzen* designs typically feature simple circular flowers *(maru-tsukushi)*, birds and landscapes, and stand out for their use of bright-coloured dyes. The technique demands great dexterity in tracing designs by hand *(tegaki)* before rice paste is applied to fabric like a stencil to prevent colours from bleeding into other areas of the fabric. By repeatedly changing the pattern of the rice paste, very complex designs can be achieved.

Together with Kyoto-dyed fabrics *(kyō-zome)*, Nishijin weaving *(Nishijin-ori)* is internationally renowned and dates to the founding of the city.

Nishijin techniques were originally developed to satisfy the demands of the nobility, who favoured the quality of illustrious silk fabrics

Washi

The art of making paper by hand was introduced to Japan from China in the 5th century and it reached its golden age in the Heian era, when it was highly prized by members of the Kyoto court for their poetry and diaries. *Washi* (traditional Japanese paper) is normally produced using mulberry, but it can also be made from mountain shrubs and other plants. One distinctive type of *washi* found in Kyoto is *kyō-chiyogami*, which

Tea ceremony

has traditionally been used by Japanese to wrap special gifts.

Tea Ceremony

Despite all the mystery surrounding it, the tea ceremony is, at heart, simply a way of welcoming a guest with a cup of tea. In Japan, this ritual has been developed and practised for almost 500 years and is properly known as *chadō* (literally, 'the way of tea'). Of course, as with most *dō* (ways) in Japan, the practice has been ritualised and formalised to an almost unimaginable

degree. In a typical tea ceremony, both the host and the guests follow a strict set of rules that vary according to the particular school of tea to which the host belongs.

Club Ōkitsu Kyoto Tea ceremony and kimono dressing in a Japanese villa. (p104)

Nishijin Kyoto's traditional textile-weaving district filled with traditional townhouses. (p97)

Kyoto International Manga Museum Get an insight into manga culture at this in-depth museum. (p46)

Camellia Tea Experience Learn the art of the tea ceremony. (p69)

Fureai-Kan Kyoto Museum of Traditional Crafts Check out displays on traditional arts and crafts. (p83)

Orinasu-kan A small museum showcasing Nishijin textiles. (p103)

Funaoka Onsen Enjoy the relaxing cultural experience of an onsen. (p104)

Haru Cooking Class Learn how to whip up your favourite Japanese dishes. (p104)

Best
Drinking & Nightlife

SHINARI/SHUTTERSTOCK ©

Kyoto and Osaka have endless options for drinking; whether it's an expertly crafted single-origin coffee in a hipster cafe, a rich *matcha* (powdered green tea) at a traditional tearoom, carefully crafted cocktails and single malts in a sophisticated six-seater bar, or Japanese craft beer in a brewery.

Where to Drink

Kyoto has a much deeper nightlife scene than what might first appear on the surface. Many bars are tucked away, hard to find and not obvious when wandering down streets and laneways. One exception is the main nightlife strip, Kiyamachi-dōri, where there's no shortage of watering holes on offer – everything from rough-and-ready student hangouts to impossibly chic spots.

Osakans love to let loose: the city is teeming with *izakaya* (pubs), bars and nightclubs. In the summertime, rooftop beer gardens set up atop department stores. Check Kansai Scene (www.kansaiscene.com) for nightclub information.

What to Drink

Beer is the overwhelming favourite as the drink to have with dinner, but gone are the days of simply having the well-known brands, Asahi, Sapporo, Kirin etc, on the menu. Craft beer is changing the beer landscape in Kyoto and Osaka, with breweries and bars specialising in craft beer popping up all over the place.

While beer is the popular choice, sake (Nihon-shu) is making a comeback in Kyoto. It's especially popular with sushi, *kaiseki* (Japanese haute cuisine) and at *izakayas*. Sake is usually consumed cold in Japan, especially the good stuff, but at more casual places like *izakaya* and *yakitori* restaurants, some people order it hot (the Japanese word for this is *atsukan*). Nondrinkers usually order oolong-cha (a smoky brown Chinese-style tea) at restaurants and almost every place stocks this. At some high-end Japanese restaurants and almost all Western ones, wine will be on the menu, the variety increasing with the quality of the restaurant. Finally, after dinner, in addition to beer, wine and sake, you'll find the full range of cocktails and spirits served in Kyoto and Osaka's myriad bars.

Dōtombori (p110), Osaka

Upmarket Bars, Kyoto

Bar K6 Single malts and expertly mixed cocktails are the draw at this smart local gathering spot. (p43)

Tōzan Bar The basement bar at the Hyatt Regency Kyoto is worth a trip for the design alone. (p71)

Gion Finlandia Bar Sophisticated Gion den with bow-tied bartenders. (p72)

Upmarket Bars, Osaka

Windows on the World Classy bar on the 35th-floor of the Hilton. (p136)

Craft Beer, Kyoto

Bungalow Cool industrial downtown bar with great beer. (p50)

Kyoto Brewing Company Great little standing-room-only tasting room. (p31)

Tadg's Gastro Pub Both expats and Japanese frequent this welcoming spot near Downtown Kyoto. (p43)

Craft Beer, Osaka

Beer Belly Osaka's best microbrewery. (p134)

Craft Beer Base Bottle shop/bar with a great range of craft beer. (p136)

Clubs, Kyoto & Osaka

World, Kyoto Huge club with a calendar of events. (p43)

Circus, **Osaka** In the centre of the city's underground electronica scene. (p119)

Best
Museums

When you tire of temple-hopping in Kyoto and bar-hopping in Osaka, there are plenty of top-rate museums to keep you entertained. Check out steam locomotives in Kyoto and oriental ceramics in Osaka, and hit all of the art galleries in between.

COWARDLION/SHUTTERSTOCK ©

Kyoto Railway Museum Kids and trainspotters will love this interactive museum. (p29)

Museum of Kyoto Check out the exhibitions and reconstruction of a typical merchant area. (p46)

Kyoto National Museum Don't miss the city's premier art museum. (p67)

Fureai-Kan Kyoto Museum of Traditional Crafts Displays of traditional crafts and arts. (p83)

National Museum of Modern Art, Kyoto Has an excellent collection of ceramics and attracts top-class art exhibitions. (p85)

Kyoto Municipal Museum of Art Major exhibitions and lovely pond out back. (p85)

Orinasu-kan, Kyoto A good overview of Nishijin textile craft. (p103)

Museum of Oriental Ceramics, Osaka Around 400 Asian ceramic pieces on display. (p131)

National Museum of Art, Osaka 20th-century art in an architecturally interesting building. (pictured above; p132)

Best Temples & Shrines

JULIANS2000/SHUTTERSTOCK ©

Kyoto's temples and shrines are the main draw for many visitors to the city, and for good reason: they are among the best examples of religious architecture on earth. With over 1000 Buddhist temples and more than 400 Shintō shrines, exploring these wonders is the work of a lifetime. Osaka also has a couple of shrines and temples worth visiting.

Temples, Kyoto

Nanzen-ji A pleasant temple complex with expansive grounds. (p76)

Kinkaku-ji The 'Golden Pavilion's' reflection shimmers in its own pond. (p90)

Ginkaku-ji The 'Silver Pavilion' has stunning Zen gardens. (p78)

Chion-in A massive complex with impressive halls and artworks. (p60)

Shoren-in One to escape the crowds and meditate overlooking the stunning garden. (p66)

Eikan-do Superb temple with city views from its pagoda. (p82)

Daitoku-ji A collection of Zen temples and perfect gardens. (p100)

Kiyomizu-dera One of the city's most popular temples. (p58)

Temples, Osaka

Hōzen-ji An urban temple covered in moss. (p116)

Shrines, Kyoto

Fushimi Inari-Taisha Hundreds of *torii* gates spread over a mountainside. (p24)

Kamigamo-jinja A shrine that predates the founding of Kyoto. (pictured above; p103)

Yasaka-jinja Shinto shrine in Gion. (p66)

Shrines, Osaka

O-hatsu Ten-jin A 1300-year-old shrine hidden among skyscrapers. (p132)

Worth a Trip

Located high on a thickly wooded mountain about 30 minutes north of Kyoto, **Kurama-dera** is one of the few temples in modern Japan that still manages to retain an air of real spirituality. This is a magical place that gains a lot of its power from its brilliant natural setting. The entrance to the temple is just up the hill from Kurama Station. A tram runs back and forth to the top for ¥100 each way, or you can hike up in about 30 minutes (follow the path past the tram station). Take the Eizan line from Demachiyanagi Station to Kurama.

ABDERAZZAK TISSOUKAI/500PX ©

Best
For Free

You may think that the cost of sightseeing in Kyoto is going to require taking a second mortgage on your home. Luckily there's plenty you can do for free — you could fill at least a week with activities that won't cost a penny. Here are just a few.

Temples

Nanzen-ji The sprawling grounds of this superb Northern Higashiyama temple make it a favourite for a stroll. (p76)

Chion-in You can tour the grounds at this immense temple complex for free. (p60)

Tōfuku-ji At the south end of the Higashiyama Mountains, this fine Zen temple has expansive grounds. (p28)

Hōnen-in There is a gallery in one of the halls that often has free art exhibits. (p82)

Shrines

Fushimi Inari-Taisha The only money you're likely to drop here is to buy a drink after climbing the mountain. (p24)

Shimogamo-jinja Take a stroll through the magnificent Tadasu-no-Mori (Forest of Truth) that leads to the main hall. (p101)

Yasaka-jinja This popular shrine is highly recommended in the evening, when the lanterns make it magical. (p66)

Parks

Kyoto Imperial Palace Park A treasure that many visitors to the city overlook. It has everything from baseball diamonds to carp ponds. (p96)

Maruyama-kōen Smack on the main sightseeing route, this lovely park is a great spot for a picnic. (p66)

Other Attractions

Nishiki Market It costs nothing to wander through this wonderful market. (p40)

Arashiyama Bamboo Grove Take a magical stroll around one of the most popular sights in Kyoto. (pictured above; p107)

Best
With Kids

Kyoto is great for kids. The usual worries aren't an issue in ultra-safe and spotless Japan. Your biggest challenge will be keeping your children entertained. The very things that many adults come to Kyoto to see (temples, gardens and shrines) can be a bit boring for kids.

How to Keep the Kids Happy

The best way to keep your kids happy in Kyoto is to mix your diet of traditional Japanese culture with things kids are more likely to enjoy. Fortunately, there is no shortage of child-friendly attractions in Kyoto, from game centres to parks and a steam locomotive museum. If your kids are older, you have lots of options: go on a hike in the mountains around the city, rent a bicycle and explore, or take them to youth-oriented shopping areas downtown such as Shingyōgoku shopping arcade and the Shijō-Kawaramachi shopping district.

Fushimi Inari-Taisha
Kids will be entranced by the hypnotic arcades of *torii* (entrance gates) at this sprawling Shintō shrine. (p24)

Kyoto Railway Museum
With vintage steam locomotives, this museum is a must for train-crazy kids. (pictured above; p29)

Kyoto Botanical Gardens For a picnic, a stroll or a Frisbee toss, these gardens are just the ticket. (p97)

Kyoto Imperial Palace Park this sprawling expanse of fields, trails, ponds and woods is perfect for a picnic, walk or bicycle ride. (p96)

Worth a Trip
Kaiyūkan (www.kaiyukan.com; 1-1-10 Kaigan-dōri) is among Japan's best aquariums. An 800m-plus walkway winds past displays of sea life from around the Pacific 'ring of fire': Antarctic penguins, coral-reef butterflyfish, unreasonably cute Arctic otters, Monterey Bay seals and unearthly jellyfish. Most impressive is the ginormous central tank, housing a whale shark, manta and thousands of other fish. Note there are also captive dolphins here, which some visitors may not appreciate; there is growing evidence that keeping cetaceans in captivity is harmful for the animals. To get there, take the Chuō line to Osaka-kō.

Best
Architecture & Gardens

You will find countless pockets of astonishing beauty in Kyoto: ancient temples with graceful wooden halls, traditional town houses clustered together along narrow streets, colourful Shintō shrines and, best of all, a profusion of gardens unlike anything else in Japan. Osaka may not have the beauty of Kyoto but it has some striking architecture.

HIROSHI H/SHUTTERSTOCK ©

Traditional Architecture

Traditional Japanese architecture is almost exclusively constructed of wood. Japanese carpenters were true masters, employing a complex system of joinery techniques to build large-scale wooden structures entirely without nails – some of which are still standing hundreds of years later.

Japanese Gardens

You'll encounter a few major types of gardens during your horticultural explorations.

Shūyū These 'stroll' gardens are intended to be viewed from a winding path, allowing the design to unfold and reveal itself from different vantages.

Kanshō Zen rock gardens (also known as *kare-sansui* gardens) are an example of this type of 'contemplative' garden intended to be viewed from one vantage point and designed to aid meditation.

Kaiyū The 'varied pleasures' garden has many small gardens with one or more teahouses surrounding a central pond.

Traditional Architecture

Ōkōchi Sansō, Kyoto Lavish estate with stunning house and teahouse. (p107)

Gion, Kyoto Traditional houses line this atmospheric old quarter. (p62)

Nishijin, Kyoto The city's traditional textile neighbourhood with traditional houses (p97)

Modern Architecture

Umeda Sky Building, Osaka Landmark building resembling a futuristic Arc de Triomphe. (pictured above; p131)

Kyoto Station An awe-inspiring steel-and-glass cathedral-like space. (p28)

Gardens

Tōfuku-ji, Kyoto Temple complex with spectacular garden. (p28)

Ginkaku-ji, Kyoto Sensational raked cones of white sand feature in this temple garden. (p78)

Ōkōchi Sansō, Kyoto Sprawling gardens with mountain views. (p107)

Shōren-in, Kyoto Giant camphor trees and a stunning landscape garden await at this quiet temple. (p66)

Best
Performing Arts

Kyoto and Osaka both have a lot to offer when it comes to seeing performing arts. Kyoto is famous for its wonderful geisha dances and traditional Japanese theatre, *nō* and kabuki, while Osaka has a strong live music scene of Japanese punk and indie rock.

STANISLAV FOSENBAUER/SHUTTERSTOCK ©

Geisha Performances, Kyoto

Kyō Odori One of the best geisha dances; held between first and third Sunday in April. (p73)

Miyako Odori Mesmerising colourful performace; held throughout April. (p72)

Kitano Odori Held between 15 and 25 April at Kamishichiken Kaburen-jō Theatre.

Kamogawa Odori Held between 1 and 24 May at Ponto-chō. (p52)

Gion Odori Charming dance; held from 1 to 10 November at the Gion Kaikan Theatre.

Live Music, Osaka

Namba Bears Basement live house and BYO beer. (p121)

Hokage Small live house featuring rock, punk and noise bands. (p121)

Theatre

Osaka Nōgaku Hall Hosts *nō* (stylised dance-drama) near Hankyū Umeda Station. (p136)

Minami-za Japan's oldest kabuki theatre in the heart of Gion, Kyoto. (p72)

ROHM Theatre Kyoto Striking building hosting a range of events including ballet and *nō* theatre. (p88)

Best
Cafes & Teahouses

Kyoto is known for its high-quality green tea and the art of the ancient tea ceremony. You'll find quaint old teahouses scattered around the city where you can enjoy a cup of *matcha* and a sweet. Alongside the tearooms you'll now find almost as many modern cafes taking coffee very seriously. Osaka's coffee scene is also taking off and it's not hard to find a good brew.

Kyoto

Vermillion Espresso Bar Convenient coffee spot for Fushimi Inari-Taisha shrine. (p31)

Kaboku Tearoom Lovely tearoom attached to the famous Ippodo Tea shop. (p41)

Kasagi-ya Local favourite for tea and traditional sweets. (p70)

% Arabica Great coffee and views to boot in Arashiyama. (p107)

Kagizen Yoshifusa Old tearoom institution in the heart of Gion. (p70)

Osaka

Jun-kissa American 1940's classic American style cafe. (p119)

Mel Coffee Roasters Tiny takeaway stand with excellent single-origin brews. (p120)

Planet 3rd Comfortable Ame-Mura cafe with light meals and iPads for use. (p118)

BEYKOV MAKSIM/SHUTTERSTOCK ©

Survival Guide

Survival Guide

Before You Go

When to Go

Kyoto

°C/°F **Temp**
40/104 —
30/86 —
20/68 —
10/50 —
0/32 —
-10/14 —

Rainfall inches/mm
— 16/400
— 12/300
— 8/200
— 4/100
— 0

J F M A M J J A S O N D

➡ **Summer** (Jun-Aug)
Weather is hot and
humid, coinciding with
the rainy season, but
it's also the season for
summer festivals.

➡ **Autumn** (Sep-Nov)
October and Novem-
ber are good times to
visit, though prices and
crowds increase in Kyoto
during autumn-foliage
season (November).

➡ **Winter** (Dec-Feb)
Temperatures plummet
and you might be lucky
enough to see snow – it
can make temple-hopping
in Kyoto a chilly pursuit.

➡ **Spring** (Mar-May)
Weather is generally fan-
tastic and it's the cherry-
blossom season (late
March to early April), but
accommodation is pricey
and hard to find.

Book Your Stay

➡ Kyoto's accommoda-
tion can be booked out
in the late March to
early April cherry-blossom
season and the November
autumn-foliage season.
It can also be hard to find
rooms during Golden
Week (29 April to 5 May)
and O-bon (mid-August).

➡ Ryokan are traditional
Japanese inns, with tatami
mats on the floor and
futons instead of beds.
The best places serve
sublime Japanese cuisine,
have attentive service and
beautiful rooms, often
with garden views.

➡ Capsule hotels are
simple hotels where you
sleep in a small 'capsule'
and use shared bathing
facilities. They're fun, but
be prepared for noise.

➡ In Osaka, base yourself
in Minami for access to a
larger selection of bars,
restaurants and shops, or
in Kita for fast access to
long-distance transport.

Dos & Don'ts

Japan is famous for its etiquette, though it's not as strict as you might think (and foreign visitors are usually given a pass).

Dos

➡ Japanese typically greet each other with a slight bow, but may greet foreigners with a handshake.

➡ The Japanese are famous queuers, forming neat lines in front of subway doors, ramen shops etc.

➡ Many lodgings and restaurants (and even some museums!) request you leave your shoes at the door. Just take a quick look around – for a sign or slippers in the foyer – to see if this rule applies.

Don'ts

➡ Hugging and cheek-kissing as a greeting is not the done thing.

➡ Eating and drinking on streets and subway cars is generally frowned upon; beverages in resealable containers are an exception.

➡ Never wear shoes on tatami mats.

➡ There is no dress code for visiting a shrine or temple but it's polite to keep your voice down.

➡ You'll find the best range of budget hotels and hostels in Kyoto around the Kyoto Station area.

Useful Websites

Lonely Planet (www. lonelyplanet.com/japan/ hotels) Recommendations and bookings.

Japan Youth Hostels (www.jyh.or.jp) Find a range of hostels in Kyoto and Osaka.

Best Budget

Tour Club (www.kyotojp. com) Well-run and welcoming guesthouse in Kyoto.

Lower East 9 Hostel (www.lowereastnine. com) Mid-century furniture and spacious capsule dorms in Kyoto.

K's House Kyoto (www. kshouse.jp) This is an international-style backpackers' favourite.

Hostel 64 Osaka (www. hostel64.com) Stylish hostel with retro furniture and a cafe/bar.

U-en (www.hostelosaka. com) Guesthouse inside an old restored townhouse in Osaka.

Best Midrange

Ibis Styles Kyoto Station (www.ibis.com) Excellent-value business hotel right next to Kyoto Station.

Royal Park Hotel The Kyoto (www.rph-the. co.jp) Smart business hotel in an unbeatable location.

Hotel Sunroute Kyoto (www.sunroute.jp) Incredible value and a great location near Downtown Kyoto.

Kaneyoshi Ryokan (www.kaneyosi.jp) Old favourite inn in the heart of Dōtombori, Osaka.

Arietta Hotel (www.the hotel.co.jp) Welcoming hotel a short walk from Minami in Osaka.

Best Top End

Tawaraya (📞075-211-5566) One of the finest ryokan in Japan, located in Downtown Kyoto.

Ritz-Carlton Kyoto (www.ritzcarlton.com) True luxury, incredible location and great views.

Hoshinoya Kyoto (http://kyoto.hoshinoya.com/en) Elegant villa-style accommodation surrounded by nature in Arashiyama – accessed by private boat!

Cross Hotel Osaka (www.crosshotel.com/osaka) Urban design hotel in unbeatable central location.

Arriving in Kyoto

Kansai International Airport

Most foreign visitors arrive in Kyoto via Kansai International Airport (KIX).

JR Haruka Airport Express The fastest and most convenient way to move between KIX and Kyoto is the special JR Haruka airport express (reserved/unreserved ¥3370/2850, 75 minutes).

Kansai International Airport Limousine Bus (📞075-682-4400; 1-way adult/child ¥2550/1280) Runs frequent buses between Kyoto and KIX (¥2550, about 90 minutes). In Kyoto, the buses depart from opposite the south side of Kyoto Station, in front of Avanti department store and Hotel Keihan.

Kyoto Station

Shinkansen (bullet trains) from Tokyo to Kyoto Station take about 2½ hours and cost around ¥13,080 for an unreserved seat. There are also *shinkansen* from cities such as Hiroshima, Osaka, Nagoya and Yokohama.

Osaka International Airport (Itami)

Osaka International Airport, commonly known as Itami (ITM), is closer to Kyoto than KIX, but it

Kansai Thru Pass

The Kansai Thru Pass is a real bonus for travellers who plan to do a fair bit of exploration in the Kansai area. It enables you to ride on city subways, private railways and city buses in Kyoto, Nara, Osaka, Kobe, Koyasan and Wakayama. It also entitles you to discounts at many attractions in the Kansai area. A two-day pass costs ¥4000 and a three-day pass costs ¥5200. It is available at the Kansai International Airport travel counter on the 1st floor of the arrivals hall and at the main bus information centre in front of Kyoto Station, among other places. For more information, visit www.surutto.com/tickets/kansai_thru_english.html.

Kyoto Bus & Subway Passes

To save time and money you can buy a *kaisū-ken* (book of five tickets) for ¥1000. There's also a *shi-basu Kyoto-bus ichinichi jōsha-ken kādo* (one-day card) valid for unlimited travel on Kyoto City buses and Kyoto buses (these are different companies) that costs ¥500. A similar pass *(Kyoto kankō ichinichi jōsha-ken)* that allows unlimited use of the bus and subway costs ¥1200. A *Kyoto kankō futsuka jōsha-ken* (two-day bus/subway pass) costs ¥2000.

Kaisū-ken can be purchased directly from bus drivers. The other passes and cards can be purchased at major bus terminals, at the bus information centre at Kyoto Station or the **Kyoto Tourist Information Center** (京都総合 観光案内所, TIC; ☎075-343-0548; 2F Kyoto Station Bldg, Shimogyō-ku; ⏰8.30am-7pm; Ⓢ Karasuma line to Kyoto). Also consider the Kansai Thru Pass.

handles only domestic traffic.

Osaka Airport Transport (☎06-6844-1124; www.okkbus.co.jp/en; 1-way ¥1310) Runs frequent airport limousine buses between Itami and Kyoto Station (55 minutes). There are less-frequent pick ups and drop offs at some of Kyoto's main hotels. The Itami stop is outside the arrivals hall – buy your ticket from the machine near the bus stop and ask one of the attendants which stand is for Kyoto. The Kyoto Station stop is in front of Avanti department store, which is opposite the south side of the station.

Arriving in Osaka

Kansai International Airport

KIX is well connected to the city with direct train lines and buses.

Nankai Express Rapit

All-reserved, twice-hourly service (7am to 10pm, ¥1430, 40 minutes) between Nankai Kansai-Airport Station (in Terminal 1) and Nankai Namba Station; Nankai Airport Express trains take about 10 minutes longer and cost ¥920. To reach Nankai Kansai-Airport Station from Terminal 2, you will need to take the shuttle bus to Terminal 1.

JR Haruka Kansai-Airport

Express Twice-hourly service (6.30am to 10pm) between KIX and Tennōji Station (unreserved seat ¥1710, 30 minutes) and Shin-Osaka Station (¥2330, 50 minutes). More-frequent JR Kansai Airport rapid trains also run between KIX, Tennōji Station (¥1060, 50 minutes) and Osaka Station (¥1190, 68 minutes); the last train departs at 11.30pm. All these stations connect to the Midō-suji subway line. It departs from Terminal 1; you need to take a free shuttle bus if you arrive at Terminal 2.

Osaka Travel Passes

Enjoy Eco Card (エンジョイエコカード; weekday/weekend ¥800/600, child ¥300) One-day unlimited travel on subways, city buses and Nankō Port Town line, plus some admission discounts. At subway ticket machines, push the 'English' button, insert cash, select 'one-day pass' or 'one-day pass weekend'.

Osaka Amazing Pass (大阪周遊パス; www.osaka-info.jp/osp) Foreign visitors to Japan can purchase one-day passes (¥2300), good for travel on city subways and trains and admission to 28 sights (including Osaka-jō and the Umeda Sky Building); or two-day passes (¥3000) that cover the same sights but only travel on city subways. Passes are sold at tourist information centres and city subway stations.

Osaka International Airport (Itami)

Itami handles domestic air travel.

Osaka Monorail Connects the airport to Hotarugaike (¥200, three minutes) and Senri-Chūō (¥330, 12 minutes), from where you can transfer, respectively, to the Hankyū Takarazaka line or Hankyū Senri line for Osaka Station.

Osaka Aiport Limousine (www.okkbus. co.jp) Frequent buses connect the airport with Osaka Station (¥640, 25 minutes), Osaka City Air Terminal (OCAT; ¥640, 35 minutes) in Namba and Shin-Osaka Station (¥500, 25 minutes). At Itami, buy your tickets from the machine outside the arrivals hall.

Shin-Osaka Station

Shin-Osaka Station is on the Tōkaidō-Sanyō *shinkansen* line (between Tokyo and Hakata in Fukuoka) and the eastern terminus of the Kyūshū shinkansen to Kagoshima. Departures are frequent.

Destinations include Tokyo (¥14,140, three hours), Hiroshima (¥10,230, 1½ hours), Hakata (¥15,000, three hours) and Kagoshima (¥21,900, 4¾ hours).

Getting Around

Subway

➡ Kyoto has two efficient subway lines, operating from 5.30am to 11.30pm. Minimum adult fare is ¥210 (children ¥110).

➡ The quickest way to travel between the north and south of Kyoto is the Karasuma subway line, and for east–west take the Tōzai subway line.

➡ In Osaka, the JR Kanjō-sen – the Osaka loop line – makes a circuit south of JR Osaka Station, though most sights fall in the middle of it.

➡ There are eight subway lines in Osaka, but the

one that short-term visitors will find most useful is the Midō-suji (red) line, running north–south and stopping at Shin-Osaka, Umeda (next to Osaka Station), Shinsaibashi, Namba and Tennōji stations. Single rides cost ¥180 to ¥370 (half-price for children).

Bus

➡ Bus entry is usually through the back door and exit is via the front door.

➡ Inner-city buses charge a flat fare (¥230 for adults, ¥120 for children aged six to 12, free for those younger), which you drop into the clear plastic receptacle on top of the machine next to the driver on your way out.

➡ Many of the routes used by visitors have announcements in English.

➡ Most buses run between 7am and 9pm, though a few run earlier or later.

➡ In addition to the regular city buses, Kyoto now has a hop-on, hop-off sightseeing bus, **K'Loop** (www.kyoto-lab.jp/kloop; adult/child 1-day pass ¥2300/1000, 2-day pass

¥3500/1000), travelling around the city's World Heritage Sites.

Bicycle

➡ Many guesthouses hire or lend bicycles to their guests and there are also hire shops around Kyoto Station, in Arashiyama and in Downtown Kyoto. With a decent bicycle and a good map, you can easily make your way all around the city.

➡ **Hub Chari** (☑070-5436-2892; http://hubchari-english.jimdo.com; per hr/day ¥200/1000) rents city bikes at several stations around Osaka. It's run by an NGO that supports Osaka's homeless community.

Taxi

➡ Taxis are a convenient, but expensive, way of getting from place to place about town.

➡ They are usually your only option after midnight, when public transport shuts down.

➡ A taxi can usually be flagged down in most parts of the city at any time. There are also a large number of *takushī noriba* (taxi stands) in

town, outside most train/subway stations, department stores etc.

➡ There is no need to touch the back doors of the cars at all – the opening/closing mechanism is controlled by the driver.

Essential Information

Business Hours

Banks 9am to 3pm Monday to Friday

Bars 7pm to late, closed one day per week

Companies 9am to 5pm or 6pm Monday to Friday

Department stores 10am to 8pm or 9pm

Post offices local 9am to 5pm Monday to Friday; central post offices 9am to 7pm Monday to Friday and 9am to 3pm Saturday

Restaurants 11am to 2pm and 6pm to 11pm, closed one day per week (often Monday or Tuesday)

Shops 9am to 5pm, may be closed Sunday

Electricity

Type A
100V/60Hz

The Japanese electric current is 100V AC. Kyoto and Osaka are on 60Hz.
Both transformers and plug adaptors are readily available in Kyoto and Osaka's big department stores such as Yodobashi Camera or Bic Camera.

Emergency

Most emergency operators don't speak English, but they will refer you to someone who does.

Ambulance & Fire (☎119)
Police (☎110)

Money

➡ The currency in Japan is the yen (¥). The Japanese pronounce yen as 'en', with no 'y' sound. The kanji for yen is: 円.

ATMs

➡ ATMs are almost as common as vending machines in Japan. Unfortunately, many do not accept foreign-issued cards.

➡ 7-Eleven stores and ATMs at most post offices accept foreign cards. These ATMs have instructions in English.

➡ 7-Eleven store ATMs are available 24 hours.

Credit Cards

➡ Note that credit cards are not as widely accepted in Japan as they are in other places – always ask in advance!

➡ Ryokan and smaller restaurants and shops are commonly cash-only.

Safe Travel

➡ Osaka has a rough image in Japan, with the highest number of reported crimes per capita of any city in the country – though it remains significantly safer than most cities of comparable size. Still, it's wise to employ the same common sense

here that you would back home. Purse snatchings are not uncommon.

➡ In Kyoto, look both ways when exiting a shop or hotel onto a pavement; there is almost always someone on a bicycle tearing your way.

Smoking

Japan has a curious policy: in many cities (including Osaka and Kyoto) smoking is banned in public spaces but allowed inside bars and restaurants. Designated smoking areas are set up around train stations. The number of smokers is declining every year.

Tourist Information

Kyoto Tourist Information Center (京都総合観光案内所, TIC; ☎075-343-0548; 2F Kyoto Station Bldg, Shimogyō-ku; ◷8.30am-7pm; Ⓢ Karasuma line to Kyoto) Stocks bus and city maps, has plenty of transport info and English speakers are available to answer your questions.

Osaka Visitors Information Center (大阪市ビジターズインフォメーションセンター・梅田; ☎06-6345-2189; www.osaka-info.jp; JR Osaka Station;

Money-Saving Tips

Sleep cheap You can find private rooms in business hotels, guesthouses and budget ryokan for as low as ¥4000 per person if you look around. If you're willing to share rooms in guesthouses or hostels, you can find beds for as low as ¥2000 per person.

Fine dine in the daytime Many of Kyoto's finest restaurants serve pared-down versions of their dinnertime fare at lunch. A *kaiseki* (Japanese haute cuisine) restaurant that can cost ¥20,000 a head at dinner might serve a lunchtime set for as little as ¥2500.

Rent a cycle Kyoto is largely flat and drivers are generally safe and courteous, making Kyoto a great city to explore on bicycle. Bike hire starts from as little as ¥500 for the day.

Buy a bus, train or subway pass Some great deals are available for Kyoto and Osaka. For more details, see the boxes on p166, p167 and p168.

Bentō bargain Skip dining in a restaurant all together and hit the local supermarket or basement food floor of department stores for cheap and filling *bentō* (boxed meals).

🕐 8am-8pm; 🚉 JR Osaka, north central exit) Umeda The main tourist office, with English information, pamphlets and maps, on the 1st floor of the central north concourse of JR Osaka Station. There are also branches on the 1st floor of Nankai Namba Station and at Kansai International Airport (KIX).

Travellers with Disabilities

➡ Larger train and subway stations have elevators, but they are not always obvious as these stations can be big and confusing.

➡ Station staff are helpful and courteous, even if most don't speak English.

➡ Most major sights have elevators or ramps and usually have a few wheelchairs to loan for use inside the facilities.

➡ Larger hotels will have one or two wheelchair-friendly rooms (it's a good idea to book in advance).

➡ Pedestrianised shopping arcades, called *shōtengai*, department store restaurant halls and mall food courts are good bets for accessible dining.

➡ **Japan Accessible** (www. japan-accessible.com/index. htm) is useful for planning.

Visas

➡ Visas are issued on arrival for most nationalities for stays of up to 90 days.

➡ Japanese law requires that visitors entering on a temporary-visitor visa possess an ongoing air or sea ticket or evidence thereof. In practice, few travellers are asked to produce such documents, but it pays to be on the safe side.

➡ On entering Japan, all short-term foreign visitors are photographed and fingerprinted.

Language

Japanese pronunciation is easy for English speakers, as most of its sounds are also found in English. Note though that it's important to make the distinction between short and long vowels, as vowel length can change the meaning of a word. The long vowels (**ā, ē, ī, ō, ū**) should be held twice as long as the short ones. All syllables in a word are pronounced fairly evenly in Japanese. If you read our pronunciation guides as if they were English, you'll be understood.

To enhance your trip with a phrasebook, visit **lonelyplanet.com**.

Basics

Hello.
こんにちは。 kon·ni·chi·wa

Goodbye.
さようなら。 sa·yō·na·ra

Yes.
はい。 hai

No.
いいえ。 ī·e

Please.
ください。 ku·da·sai

Thank you.
ありがとう。 a·ri·ga·tō

Excuse me.
すみません。 su·mi·ma·sen

Sorry.
ごめんなさい。 go·men·na·sai

How are you?
お元気ですか? o·gen·ki des ka

Fine. And you?
はい、元気です。 hai, gen·ki des
あなたは? a·na·ta wa

Do you speak English?
英語が ē·go ga
話せますか? ha·na·se·mas ka

I don't understand.
わかりません。 wa·ka·ri·ma·sen

Eating & Drinking

I'd like to reserve a table for (two).
(2人)の (fu·ta·ri) no
予約をお yo·ya·ku o
願いします。 o·ne·gai shi·mas

I'd like (the menu).
(メニュー) (me·nyū)
をお願いします。 o o·ne·gai shi·mas

I don't eat (red meat).
(赤身の肉) (a·ka·mi no ni·ku)
は食べません。 wa ta·be·ma·sen

That was delicious.
おいしかった。 oy·shi·kat·ta

Please bring the bill.
お勘定 o·kan·jō
をください。 o ku·da·sai

Cheers! 乾杯! kam·pai

beer ビール bī·ru

coffee コーヒー kō·hī

Shopping

I'd like ...
…をください。 ... o ku·da·sai

I'm just looking.
見ているだけです。 mi·te i·ru da·ke des

How much is it?
いくらですか? | i·ku·ra des ka

That's too expensive.
高すぎます。 | ta·ka·su·gi·mas

Can you give me a discount?
ディスカウント | dis·kown·to
できますか? | de·ki·mas ka

Emergencies

Help!
たすけて! | tas·ke·te

Go away!
離れろ! | ha·na·re·ro

Call the police!
警察を呼んで! | kē·sa·tsu o yon·de

Call a doctor!
医者を呼んで! | i·sha o yon·de

I'm lost.
迷いました。 | ma·yoy·mash·ta

I'm ill.
私は病 | wa·ta·shi wa
気です。 | byō·ki des

Where are the toilets?
トイレは | toy·re wa
どこですか? | do·ko des ka

Time & Numbers

What time is it?
何時ですか? | nan·ji des ka

It's (10) o'clock.
(10)時です。 | (jū)·ji des

Half past (10).
(10)時半です。 | (jū)·ji han des

morning	朝	a·sa
afternoon	午後	go·go
evening	夕方	yū·ga·ta

yesterday	きのう	ki·nō
today	今日	kyō
tomorrow	明日	a·shi·ta

1	一	i·chi
2	二	ni
3	三	san
4	四	shi/yon
5	五	go
6	六	ro·ku
7	七	shi·chi/ na·na
8	八	ha·chi
9	九	ku/kyū
10	十	jū

Transport & Directions

Where's the ...?
…はどこ | ... wa do·ko
ですか? | des ka

What's the address?
住所は何 | jū·sho wa nan
ですか? | des ka

Can you show me (on the map)?
(地図で)教えて | (chi·zu de) o·shi·e·te
くれませんか? | ku·re·ma·sen ka

When's the next (bus)?
次の(バス)は | tsu·gi no (bas) wa
何時ですか? | nan·ji des ka

Does it stop at ...?
…に | ... ni
停まりますか? | to·ma·ri·mas ka

Please tell me when we get to ...
… に着いたら | ... ni tsu·i·ta·ra
教えてください。 | o·shi·e·te ku·da·sai

Behind the Scenes

Send Us Your Feedback

We love to hear from travellers – your comments help make our books better. We read every word, and we guarantee that your feedback goes straight to the authors. Visit **lonelyplanet.com/contact** to submit your updates and suggestions.

Note: We may edit, reproduce and incorporate your comments in Lonely Planet products such as guidebooks, websites and digital products, so let us know if you don't want your comments reproduced or your name acknowledged. For a copy of our privacy policy visit lonelyplanet.com/privacy.

Kate's Thanks

A huge thank you to Destination Editor, Laura, for giving me the opportunity to work on a dream gig and for all of your assistance throughout. A big *arigatou gozaimasu* to Kengo Nakao from the Kyoto Tourist Information office for all of your help, also to Keiji Shimizu for your assistance and Motoki Ito for some great local tips. And finally, to my partner Trent, who I missed travelling with on this trip, thanks for all of your support.

Rebecca's Thanks

Much gratitude as always to my family and friends for their support, company (on many a research excursion) and patience (especially when deadlines loom). Thank you to Simon and Laura for being there with spot-on tips, suggestions, advice (and patience).

Acknowledgements

Cover photograph: Women wearing traditional kimonos, Kyoto, Maurizio Rellini/4Corners ©
Contents photograph: Kiyomizu-dera, Kyoto, P Kamput/Shutterstock ©

This Book

This 1st edition of Lonely Planet's *Pocket Kyoto & Osaka* guidebook was researched and written by Kate Morgan and Rebecca Milner. This guidebook was produced by the following:

Destination Editor
Laura Crawford

Product Editors
Carolyn Boicos, Jenna Myers

Senior Cartographer
Diana Von Holdt

Book Designer Virginia Moreno

Assisting Editors Imogen Bannister, Bruce Evans, Kristin Odijk, Amanda Williamson

Cover Researcher
Naomi Parker

Thanks to Naoko Akamatsu, Catherine Naghten, Anthony Phelan

Index

See also separate subindexes for:

⊗ Eating p177

🍺 Drinking p177

⭐ Entertainment p178

🛍 Shopping p178

Our Writers

Kate Morgan

Having worked for Lonely Planet for over a decade now, Kate has been fortunate enough to cover plenty of ground working as a travel writer on destinations such as Japan, India, Zimbabwe, the Philippines and Phuket. She has done stints living in London, Paris and Osaka, but these days is based in one of her favourite regions in the world – Victoria, Australia. In between travelling the world and writing about it, Kate enjoys spending time at home working as a freelance editor. For this edition, Kate contributed the Kyoto chapters.

Rebecca Milner

Rebecca was born in California and is now a long-time Tokyo resident (14 years and counting!). She has co-authored Lonely Planet guides to Tokyo, Japan, Korea and China, and has been published in the *Guardian*, *Independent*, *Sunday Times Travel Magazine* and *Japan Times*. After spending the better part of her twenties working to travel, Rebecca was fortunate enough to turn the tables in 2010, joining the Lonely Planet team of freelance authors. For this edition, Rebecca contributed the Osaka chapters.

Published by Lonely Planet Global Limited
CRN 554153
1st edition – Aug 2017
ISBN 978 1 78657 655 2
© Lonely Planet 2017 Photographs © as indicated 2017
10 9 8 7 6 5 4 3 2 1
Printed in China